Good Fruits

SAME-SEX RELATIONSHIPS
AND CHRISTIAN FAITH

JIM COTTER

D1392276

EXETER

❖❖❖❖❖❖❖❖❖❖❖❖❖❖❖❖❖❖❖❖❖❖❖

CAIRNS PUBLICATIONS

1988

© Copyright by Jim Cotter 1981, 1988
ISBN 1 870652 03 7

First published 1981
Second edition 1988

Further copies of this book are obtainable from

Cairns Publications
47 Firth Park Avenue, Sheffield, S5 6HF

Printed by The Devonshire Press Ltd
Printing House, Barton Road
Torquay, Devon, TQ2 7NX

CONTENTS

Preface

Seven years on

It is seven years since I put together for publication a selection of articles which had been written for the then *Gay News* under the overall title of *Our God Too*. That collection is now out of print, but the issues it raised are still pertinent. Critical friends have persuaded me that many of the original articles should still be available. They are reproduced here with a few amendments, as Chapters 1 to 5, with the one exception of Chapter 4.ii, which is new. Chapter 6 originally appeared as a pamphlet published by the Lesbian and Gay Christian Movement and is reproduced here with permission. It consists of the expanded text of the Michael Harding Memorial Address for 1985. Chapter 7 is substantially the same as a lecture given in April this year to launch what is in many ways a companion volume to this one, some perspectives on sexuality and spirituality entitled *Pleasure, Pain and Passion*.

I am grateful to more people than I can possibly mention who have been and continue to be companions on the painful but exhilarating exploration of what it means to be a sexual human being, especially if you provisionally describe yourself as belonging to two minority groups – gay and Christian. This book is dedicated to them.

And I do want to thank two people in particular, Norman Pittenger, whose writings on sexuality provided a rare beacon of hope more than twenty years ago, and Monica Furlong, whose writings on faith and prayer helped to keep the spirit alive and who has contributed a generous foreword to this volume.

In writing on same-sex relationships and Christian faith I think I have been seeking to enlighten, reassure, and persuade both myself and others. I believe this is no less needed now

v

than seven to ten years ago. I hope too that there is from time to time a light touch, for it is all too easy to be precious, solemn, and self-defensive on this issue. In the rest of this preface I want to reflect on what has been happening since the first edition of this book was published, again seeking meaning in perplexing events, trying to reassure the frightened (including myself), and attempting to be lightly persuasive. I am writing in the early summer of 1988.

By what authority?

The Christian Church has never been without deeply held conflicting convictions, and it is one of the tasks of those who hold office within it to create an atmosphere in which these tensions can be worked with until deeper resolutions emerge than the simplistic victory of one side over another. It is therefore a particularly unpleasant phenomenon when Christians go to court to resolve conflicts. What happens is that the deeper resolutions are thereby postponed, and self-righteousness on both sides is that much more difficult to eradicate.

The fact that the office of the Lesbian and Gay Christian Movement was in the tower of St. Botolph's Church, Aldgate, in London (and had been for ten years) without an official diocesan licence was an irregularity of canon law. By that law the headquarters of an organisation that causes controversy in the Church cannot be situated on consecrated ground. In this particular instance the office was half-way up the tower and had no direct access to the main body of the church; to reach it you had to toil up a narrow spiral staircase off the baptistery/entrance lobby. The office was hardly intrusive or offensive. Its position might have been construed not to have broken the spirit of the law – even on the supposition that the law is a just one in the first place.

To comply with canon law, a 'faculty', i.e. the official licence, was applied for. The Archdeacon of London was the sole objector, and for reasons of financial and legal prudence, the application was withdrawn. The sequence of events was much more complicated than this outline suggests, and at the time of writing the costs were still in dispute. The point here is that we have an illustration of a heavy-handed way of exercising authority, and one that was quite unnecessary, since the Lesbian and Gay Christian Movement and the Parochial Church Council of St. Botolph's had shown every willingness to discuss and come to an agreement. Of course there must be power to say No vested in some authority representing an organisation, but its use *not* as a last resort damages the credibility of that authority. It does not exactly encourage lesbian and gay people to take the authority of the Church seriously when matters of sexuality are addressed.

Nearly everyone would accept the need for some laws, some rules that protect the weak and restrain excess, especially where force against the person is concerned. But the notorious Clause 29, the bewildering variety of ages of consent in different countries in Western Europe, and the opportunities for discrimination in housing and employment do not help the secular authority to carry much weight as far as gay people are concerned.

In reaction, some people would say that the only guide, the only reliable authority for behaviour, is their own conscience. The difficulty here is that one person's conscience may tell them to do something diametrically opposite to another's, and we do in practice look for grounds for decisions which take others in a community seriously -- even in days of rank individualism. Also it is very easy for conscience to be lazy: most of us can find very good reasons for doing what we want to do.

It *may* come down to conscience in the end, but I don't think this absolves us from the task of working out *together* guidelines for the individual and common good. I emphasise 'together' for those affected by any corporate decision-making must be included in the process of that decision-making. Otherwise the rule of law quickly becomes the rule of force, exercised by the tyranny of the few. So it is vital that conflict be contained within a community. Then everyone concerned is challenged with the necessity to think deeply about how we want to live; each will be sufficiently in touch with others to put and to hear the awkward questions; and the corporate wisdom of the past can be critically and respectfully considered.

Part of that wisdom for Christian people is the kind of insight that can be discerned through the pages of the Bible, such as the priority of self-giving love, the need to work with the tensions of love and justice, of challenge and forgiveness, of power and mercy, and the warnings against behaviour that is destructive of self and community.

However, that wisdom is in parables, stories, proverbs. Where there are detailed rules, these are illustrations from the experience of a past community of how they understood the demands of the love of God in their own time. We can learn from them, but we shouldn't expect all the answers to be the same today. We are called to make our own contribution to the Christian story, and that may involve us in the kind of vulnerable risks that have to be taken if some new pattern of life is to take shape among us. Some lesbian and gay people would make the modest claim that they may be contributing in our day, through that process of risk and, often, failure, to the discernment of a new wisdom in patterns of human relationships.

The first Christians were Jewish in background. Something new of the Love of God had hit them, and it proved impossible to contain what was new in the forms of the old. They further discovered that the Gentiles had had the same experience of God's love in Christ, and it is not surprising that it took time and an agonising process of conflict and debate and prayer to admit this seemingly impossible fact. The parallel places the responsibility on our shoulders to contribute our partial awareness of the truth in an open and honest way, and to ask of those who feel troubled by us to contain their unease and not to push us away out of sight and mind.

We cannot avoid hurting and being hurt. But the enduring of the conflict in hope is for the sake of the deepest of all loves that dare to speak their name. In the end this is the only authority that counts – the authentic love that is scarred. Such love vindicates itself, it is focused decisively on Jesus of Nazareth, and it is witnessed to in the Bible, in the Church, in human experience, and in the individual conscience. It is rarely seen in courts of law.

Who holds to truth and who holds power?

There is a danger in liberal even-handedness. In the popular church mind the Lesbian and Gay Christian Movement is perceived as the polar opposite of the Association for Biblical Witness to our Nation, their respective spokesmen, Richard Kirker and Tony Higton, ranged against each other. Quotations in the press seem to play rhetoric off against rhetoric. Extreme claims are made by both sides on television: the vast majority or a minute minority of homosexual men are supposedly promiscuous. Truth collapses in the distortions of partial vision. The same political tactics of leafletting and lobbying alienate many of the thoughtful members of the General Synod of the Church of England. The temptation is to dimiss both organisations as irrational extremists.

But in calmer moments it is worth asking, How many members of the two organisations abhor slogans and simple answers to complex questions? For matters of sexuality are indeed complex, and we are all at our most vulnerable as sexual beings. It is true that out of anger and hurt some gay people seem to claim self-righteously that they are 100% in the right. But most are only too aware that there are no easy answers and are all too ready to dialogue with others who think differently – as long as they too are willing to enter the conversation in a spirit of exploration. It may be that many of the members of ABWON are willing to dialogue in this fashion, but it is the sad experience of gay people that most fundamentalist Christians are not. Each of us needs to talk with those who differ from us. And we need to decide for ourselves whose minds are most closed and whose are open to new truth.

Further, it is not necessarily the most open-minded who hold the reins of power. The two organisations are not equal in the amount of power they can wield, that power being represented by the letter of the law and the money that can be obtained by the wealthy who fear change. Not only this: members of ABWON may be offended, both personally and, it is claimed, in God's name, by same-sex activity in all circumstances, they may be hurt and angry and bewildered by challenges to sexual mores, they may withdraw their support from their local parish and join a more fundamentalist sect. But *as human beings*, on this issue they are not themselves vulnerable and hesitant, not threatened with exclusion from congregations and families and places of work. They do not themselves feel the pressure of the outcome of the General Synod's debate in November 1987 which has caused at least two priests to my knowledge to commit suicide.

So, in matters of truth and power, LGCM and ABWON are not equal partners in discussion. The tentative seekers after truth and the weaker in terms of power can open up in honesty to others only when the stronger party admit that they are stronger and repent of what they have done to those who are weaker.

Indeed a political issue

I have become more and more convinced over the last seven years that the issue of same-sex relationships is political, in both ecclesiastic and secular terms. Someone added to the old tag about power corrupting and absolute power corrupting absolutely by muttering that ecclesiastical power corrupts diabolically. Laws and policies do create a climate of discouragement or encouragement of particular patterns of individual relationships and behaviour. As a direct result gay people feel either that they are hemmed in or that they have room to breathe. When there is very little room, when there are no circumstances in which any kind of same-sex relationship can be openly acknowledged and recognized, then it is hardly surprising that it should prove difficult to establish and sustain such a relationship. The remarkable fact in the circumstances is that so many couples do survive through the years.

I was shown a letter recently which a priest had drafted to his bishop. It is a sign of the times that the letter was never sent and that it can be quoted here only anonymously. It eloquently makes this point about the pressures of a whole church and society.

"During my twenties and thirties I had two long-term relationships, both of which ended because, in different ways, my partners had experienced deep fear of the social consequences of being gay in their teenage years. In adult life they found it difficult to live with the realized dream of a settled relationship. In my situation, of course, that settled relationship had to be completely hidden beyond our circle of close trustworthy friends. My professional life obviously did not give any encouragement . . . to live in a socially supported, permanent relationship . . . So it proved very difficult to establish that commitment in love to one other person which I believe to be an almost basic human instinct . . . I personally cannot face finding another partner in the overtly sexually orientated world of the 'gay scene', itself the result, I fear, of so much rejection of gay people as *social* people. The 'ghetto' does, in fact, thrive under oppression, but the oppression produces a stifling atmosphere."

Such oppression, hidden or open, has for centuries been a feature of western society. The historian R.I.Moore, in *The Formation of a Persecuting Society, Power and Deviance in Western Europe*, 950–1250, (Basil Blackwell, 1987) has asked why it was that in the eleventh and twelfth centuries, in contrast to the immediately preceding ones, Western Europe *became* a persecuting society. One possibility he examines is that those seeking to establish power, i.e. the new clerical class in budding nation states, over against the old warrior barons in their feuding fiefdoms, created in people's imaginations the threat of the polluting and the disorderly, establishing the identity of 'heretics', 'lepers', 'sodomites', and later 'witches', none of whom could actually exercise the power that was projected on to them, and destroying the identity of the Jews, whose abilities and culture were indeed a rival to their own and may in fact have been superior to it. "Persecution became habitual. That is to say not simply that individuals were subject to violence, but that deliberate and socially sanctioned violence began to be directed, *through established governmental, judicial and social institutions,* against groups of people defined by general characteristics such as race, religion, or way of life and that membership of such groups in itself became to be regarded as justifying these attacks." (p. 5)

Politically and socially very little has changed since that time, and too many people, now the black, the disabled, the mentally handicapped, the helpless elderly, the sexually variant, the person with AIDS, all share with gay and Jewish people the sense that at the very least they do not habitually receive a dignity of treatment from their fellow human beings.

This experience was acknowledged by the Bishop of Durham in a presidential address to the Durham Diocesan Synod in May 1988: "I am quite clear that the evidence for the current putting of pressure on homosexuals and homosexual groups to a point which is persecutory is undeniable. I am sure that this is wrong and I am clear that it is evidence of a dangerous trend around to respond to the uncertainties, problems, and real dangers of our social life at present by looking for scapegoats among the 'abnormal' and the 'minorities' and taking out our own fears and worries on them."

Perhaps we are again living in a time when no one is really sure where power and authority lie. Is it with Parliament? Is it with bishops and synods? Is it with multi-national companies? Is it with those who have most information at their finger tips?

Is it with those who have access to nuclear, chemical, and biological poison, most of which is invisible? There are more authoritarian governments than ever in the world today, yet much of their rhetoric sounds hollow. Have they an authority that commends assent? Whatever the particular weight given to various answers to such questions, those who seek the mind of Christ may wish to look elsewhere and find a different kind of power at work among those whom the powerful reject. And whatever events actually occur, our value and identity as sexual beings is inevitably caught up in the processes of corporate change which are played out in the political arena. And the times we live in are not conducive to tolerance and acceptance of variety.

Signs of hope

Nevertheless, I refuse to be pessimistic, however tight the situation facing gay people today. There are signs of hope. There is considerable intelligent comment from those in the Church who have no vested interest, who could hardly be accused of 'promoting' (what a giveaway word for a society greedy for more possessions and where everything seems to be reduced to privatised sales) homosexuality. Those of us who want to help people to keep, in their mind's eye, human beings and their relationships rather than particular genital acts, are encouraged to read of those who, while finding anal intercourse emotionally repellent, refuse to allow that feeling to dictate their attitudes. The recently retired Bishop of Birmingham, Hugh Montefiore, has written in *The Times* in February 1988 that he has come to terms with that emotional reaction and it no longer influences his opinion. In the address already quoted, the Bishop of Durham said, in his usual forthright manner, "I do know enough about myself, about psychology and the general observation of personal behaviour and about God's open and risky way of pressing His commandments, judgments and offers of love, to be aware that when strong feelings at 'gut-level' are aroused then we need a great

deal of mutual help, readiness for self-reflection and develop-
ment of sensitivity if we are to proceed in a humane way which
is appropriately related to godliness." He further went on to
say, ". . . it is normal for a certain percentage of people to be
'abnormal'. Of course, they will always be a minority but they
are *not* unnatural nor in any moral or human sense, ab-normal.
Now, we have not yet learnt socially or in the Church how to
respond to this with any firmness, clarity, or ease. It is a
learning we have to do, a groaning we have to go through, and a
part of our movement towards the Future which is 'on the
move' in a way which is particularly disturbing and unsettling
for very many of us."

So he is asking for the kind of exploration that might have
been expected to have resulted from the publication of the
Gloucester Report of 1979, *Homosexual Relationships*, which was
at the time shelved. That report recognized that there were
Christians who "held (on solid theological grounds) that an
active homosexual relationship in the context of fidelity and
promise was a possible lifestyle for believers." So Rowan
Williams, a professor of divinity at Oxford, has reminded us,
and he went on to say in a statement about the Diocese of
London's action against the office of the Lesbian and Gay
Christian Movement: "Christians should be able to live with a
continuing discussion on such a matter in which all are
prepared to share insights out of the common Christian
heritage, and these insights are less clear and absolute on this
than is often claimed."

Another sign of hope is the ready availability of serious
literature, fiction and non-fiction, in ordinary bookshops – a
situation very different from fifteen years ago. In fiction alone
there have been novels and short stories by such writers as
David Leavitt, Edmund White, Alan Hollinghurst, and
Andrew Harvey, and there has been a flow of interesting work
from the Gay Men's Press and from the burgeoning women's
presses. Among magazines, there is the weighty *European Gay
Journal*, the substantial *Advocate* in the United States and *Gay*

Pied in France, and the more popular *Gay Times* in this country. Further, there is the network of local gay groups, as well as the telephone Gay Switchboard, and the various responsible self-help and counselling organisations, not least in this time of AIDS, the Terrence Higgins Trust. Of course not all Christians would agree with all the opinions put forward and all the patterns of behaviour described or advocated, but the point I want to make here is that the material for debate is widely available, and that there need no longer be the terror of hollow isolation that was the lot of so many gay people not so long ago, and in places and in certain countries alas still is.

Cautiously, I would even venture the suggestion that the noise being created by conservatives and evangelicals is not all loss. The very fact of its vociferousness may be an indication that there is more strength around in gay circles now than we sometimes imagine. Certainly, the noise is that of tired cliché and outworn myths. However, I do not underestimate the power of myths in the human heart, and it can easily overcome the saner voices, like that of the Roman Catholic psychiatrist, Jack Dominian, who is ready to conduct a serious conversation about the ways in which our understanding of the purposes of human sexuality is changing. We cannot go back to the time when sexuality was understood solely in terms of necessary procreation and fitful passion. So I refuse to be too downcast. So many people have now become aware that there are ordinary, if unusual, men and women in their midst, in their congregations and families and places of work. Even if the more public doors of openness have clanged shut for a while, there is much more quiet acceptance and understanding. It is still a minority of opinion in the population, though in the days immediately before the AIDS panic some surveys of public opinion were showing a majority accepting. If I am not all the time optimistic, I am not pessimistic either. I remain hopeful of creative change, and am aware of many courageous people paying their portion of the painful cost of such change.

JIM COTTER, *June* 1988

Foreword

In the time I grew up the word 'gay' had never, so far as I know, been spoken in connection with sexual orientation, and the word 'homosexual' was not one which often, or perhaps ever, occurred in my adolescent conversation. Of course, I knew that there were girls at the school I went to who loved other girls – well, *all* of us, I seem to remember, were in love with other girls at times, but for some it seemed to go deeper and to matter more than for others. No one pinned a label on the habit, though teachers did seem to grow inexplicably worried about it, but I took it quite naturally as one of those odd things girls did. We thought neither better nor worse of those who did it.

It was only in my late teens when I began to read more adult novels that one or two of them began to hint at a mysterious male habit . . . For a long while I couldn't make out what they were on about, and when I did, could not see what all the fuss was about (and never have since, I may say). Sex was relatively harmless, wasn't it? At least for a girl who had grown up in a world of air-raids and concentration camps and who had matriculated in the year of Hiroshima, it was difficult to feel too shocked at the idea of people, any two people, making love together.

I quickly discovered, however, that I was in a world that did not see it as I did. One of my closest and dearest male friends was, I eventually realized, homosexual in orientation. It was part of the tragedy of the times that it was many many years before he could ever discuss it with me, and when he did tell me it was to say how deeply hurt he had been by the society in which he grew up. He had been a faithful Christian, and had faithfully followed the teachings of the Church about the celibacy necessary for homosexuals, only to feel in late middle age that he was desperately lonely and frustrated and that he bitterly regretted the choice that had been forced upon him. I sensed his unhappiness long before he ever told me about it, but was as inhibited as he was about bringing the subject up. It simply was not something to be talked about, at least between a man and a woman.

In the early sixties, working as a journalist in Fleet Street, I began to look again at the way society considered homosexuality, in those few years of intensive debate that led up to the Homosexual Law Reform Act of 1967. By then I perfectly well knew that many men and women, some of whom I deeply admired for their contributions to the world of art, literature, the theatre, music, thought, religion, were not physically attracted to people of the opposite sex, however much they might enjoy their company. It disgusted me that any detective with nothing better to do might turn one of them in — at least in the case of the men. But it disgusted me just as much that many men who were not famous at all were desperately vulnerable to policemen, blackmailers and those who simply resented their existence. About 1965 I remember a young man coming to see me at the *Daily Mail* to see if I could help him (I had already begun to write articles attacking the existing homosexual laws). Relatives had lent him money to start a restaurant and he was searching for a suitable site when he went into a London pub, well-known for its homosexual clientele, for a few drinks. While there, in a totally naïve way he allowed compromising photographs to be taken of him, but was so innocent that it was not until several days later when copies were sent to him, with threats to tell his relatives and his present employer if he did not hand over several thousand pounds, that he realized the risk he had run. It is almost impossible now to remember the kind of terror in which gay people then lived, the fear of mentioning their sexuality to non-gay friends, the painful pretences and lies and loneliness.

Many older gays who grew up in that cruel and uncomprehending world still carry the memory of those humiliating deceptions, and some are so damaged that they remain as much 'in the closet' as ever; but one of the joys of the past fourteen years has been to see the gradual relaxation of fear in the gay community, the cheerful courage of those 'coming out', the sturdy good sense of *Gay News*, the re-education of 'straights' or heterosexuals into new, more realistic ways of thought. Not that the struggle is over – there are many bigots about, many, even within the gay community, who find homosexuality repugnant and frightening in a totally irrational way, many heterosexuals who have still not quite caught up with changes of thought and who imagine that to be homosexual is to be a peculiar oddity, a corrupter of others, or a traitor to one's country.

Well, it's not, and as more and more gays have 'come out' many have made the important discovery that except in one (important) particular gays are just like everyone else. Not that there's any particular reason that they *should* be like everyone else – heterosexuals are not usually so colourful or so fulfilled that they specially inspire imitation – but the fact is that for the most part gays and non-gays are indistinguishable, and the old divisions have more to do with our fantasies, rather like racialist fantasies, than with profound differences.

However, there is still a long process of education to be completed, in which non-gays have to think more deeply about their fantasies and about their unthinking attitudes to homosexuality (which still cause pain), and in which gays have to go with the sometimes costly process of recovering the self-esteem that centuries of either silence or persecution took away, of learning that it is safe to 'come out' and simply be themselves.

It is this process which Jim Cotter's book (and even more, Jim Cotter himself) encourages in a quite remarkable way. Reprinting his pieces from *Gay News* – pieces which tackled, issue by issue, the subjects which were talking-points for gays as the months went by – he touches on many sensitive places, and does it with real knowledge and honesty and love. I have talked pretty freely with gay friends for some years now, but even so I learned a good deal from his book – about the kind of unthinking comments from non-gays which make it all harder, about the anger well-meaning religious groups induce in the gay community, about the long struggle for many men and women to break out of loneliness and begin to trust in a world which has not shown very much love or understanding. Once or twice I was desperately moved.

Gays will also like the book, however, since it sets out arguments, points of view, new ways of coming at old chestnuts, in a way that is clear, interesting and often witty. The book deserves to sell, and I hope it will. I hope too that it may be the first of other books by Jim Cotter which will explore the sexual fears and doubts of our puzzled society in ever greater depth. We all have a great deal to learn, but perhaps we could adopt Jim's book as a kind of first text-book until we are ready to go on to the more difficult lessons that I suspect he is already ready to teach us.

Life is about living and letting live, and also about loving and letting love, however hard some people find it to give others this kind of permission, and what Jim's book does above all is to say something true and profound about loving. Good on it.

MONICA FURLONG
1981

I
Words

I. WHOSE WORDS?

"I've never had any reason to think he's anything but normal." So said a woman in the middle of asking me a question after I'd tried to 'tell it the way it is' for an hour. Anger fought with weariness. "Don't you understand – the words you've just used say so much. Don't you see the insult? All right, I know that you think the word is shorthand, and I know you've just said that you've become much more tolerant as you've grown older . . ."

'Normal' is a word we're so familiar with, often over a lifetime, but it's part of a language of oppression. It's hard to see that 'normal' usually means 'that which we're most comfortable with.' Very hard to realize – even more so to act on that realization – that definitions are shaped by the powerful and articulate and used to devalue the oppressed and the silent.

The 'normal' define themselves and in turn define the 'abnormal' or 'deviant'; the 'married' define and classify others as 'un-married', 'separated', 'divorced', 'widowed', even 'single' (to which a variant is presumably, "No, I'm double.")

It's the same with the 'disabled' – those who do not have or who have lost an 'ability'. They are 'not-able', often thought of as useless, and a burden to the community. The arrogant Christian does the same when talking about non-Christians, the racist when talking about non-whites – let alone the husband who has 'taken a wife' and gives her his surname, which she carries even after he's died. And I guess most people still see homosexuality as a sickness, defined by the 'norm' of healthy heterosexuality. Nor is it long since gay people (now self-defined from within the experience of once silenced human beings) were defined solely by reference to one male sexual act – buggers, sodomites. (Similarly, to talk about disability is often to focus on an isolated limb rather than on the whole person.)

The trouble is that we hate giving up the idea that somewhere there are 'perfectly normal' people, that we are – or once were – perfect. It's an illusion that starts very early. "Thank God he's perfect", say the parents anxious about a possible genetic defect and now relieved that their baby is without 'blemish'. (Incidentally, the word 'their' is often used to mean, 'that which belongs to us, our possession' rather than a new being temporarily entrusted to their care.)

I don't believe there ever was a perfect Paradise, unless that word refers to the blissful state of untroubled waters in the very early months after conception. There was no 'Fall' from perfection, either for the individual or for the species.

True, we know that we are less than we have it in us to become. I think that is because we have all been hurt and we either seek revenge in rage or retreat into ourselves through fear, and so refuse to be drawn into the future. In that sense, we are incomplete and yearn for completion, while resisting it at the same time. We strike discordant notes on the way towards resolution and harmony. The point is that the future matters more than that past, and that we are all facing the same direction – human beings as yet incomplete, each with a unique mixture of inherited and environmental raw material. (I gather that the word 'handicap' comes from the phrase 'hand in the cap', i.e. drawing out a lottery ticket, the card dealt to you by Fate.)

The powerful and the wealthy are usually the most afraid and the most unwilling to admit these things. At least the oppressed and the silenced know, once they refuse to collude. But it is hard to escape this language trap. The OED refers to a hospital set up in 1597 for the "halt, the crooked, and the stigmatic" – the shift in meaning of these words indicates how easily the not so agile were seen as near neighbours to the criminal and the outcast. That is a long way from saying that the not so agile and the not so clever may have more opportunity than most of us to become still and wise. If my face is scarred, do I become bitter that I've lost my looks, or can I bear my incompleteness, my woundedness, transforming it by being drawn, not to a state of perfection, but to a maturity of love?

Meanwhile, I am incomplete. And I also want to say that I may well be 'exceptional' in certain ways in contrast to the 'usual', a 'cut above the average'; and if I am not 'familiar' to you, I may be your 'unfamiliar spirit' holding a mirror to what disturbs you in yourself. If we should meet in the street, recognize yourself.

II. THE LAMBETH HANDICAP

Wonderful! We have a new word to play with – Handicapped! At last I can do what I've always wanted – park on double yellow lines with my 'Disabled' sticker on the rear windscreen. (It's pink, of course, and triangular in shape.)

I owe that delicious thought to a letter in *The Guardian*. Another on the same day quoted part of the Oxford English Dictionary's definition of handicap: "the extra weight to be carried by the *superior* horse" (my italics). Always knew there was something special about being gay! I've felt like a racehorse all week.

So the Archbishop of Canterbury, commendably searching for new words to avoid the old categories of sin, crime, and sickness (the first three hurdles in the race!), introduced us to the notion of handicap in the debate on Homosexual Relationships in the General Synod of the Church of England.

Well, it's *better* . . . and many people will think it so *nearly* right . . . I mean, we can at least make political use of the phrase. After all, the archibishop said that people should respect the handicapped and be willing to learn from them. I shall enjoy using the bidding prayer, "Let us pray for the handicapped, that we may respect them and learn from them." Even the editorial in the *Sunday Telegraph* may not have been wholly on the wrong lines in wondering if the archbishop now thought homosexuality "a blessing in disguise". And yes, the language of handicap allows one to talk of justice more than of compassion, of a problem of society more than that of the individual. And indeed it will always be an effort (often a very creative one) for particular individuals or groups with special gifts to make their contribution to the life of a society where the majority of people do not want to listen.

But we don't need the active oppression of that majority to make things doubly difficult. Here's another definition from the Oxford English Dictionary: to handicap: "to place anyone at a disadvantage by the imposition of any embarrassment, impediment, or disability." And too many people draw back from a one-eyed person in terror, or at best come close in pity.

If you're a 'masculine male' and are married with three or four children and find your sexual life satisfying, then anything *other* than that is bound to seem to be something *less* than that. And what *seems* a handicap to the majority of people then comes to be *defined* as such. As the press statement from the Gay Christian Movement put it, gay people are categorized by such definitions as "less than whole, lacking in something essential, and not having true validity."

The person so defined may decide to play along: after all, there is a long tradition of such divisions in society – conformist and nonconformist, king (powerful) and jester (weak fool), healthy and crippled, the rich man in his castle and the poor man at his gate. If you are one of the minority and accept your place, the rewards can be substantial (for a few), even in terms of what once was quaintly called 'preferment' in the Church of England.

During the debate in the General Synod, the Revd Bob Lewis of Thirsk 'came out' – a brave and courageous act which deservedly earned him prolonged applause. But *at the same time* as refusing to collude with the conspiracy of *silence* –

and this is what makes it all so subtle and difficult – he endorsed the conspiracy of 'This is something I should prefer to be without.' He used the language of 'disability' and 'cheat' to describe his sexuality. I do not doubt his sincerity, but I do question the perception. And when he finished by saying that he held this 'mystery' before God every day from his 'dunghill', I wondered if the loud applause was partly expressing the conviction that sex and the feelings linked with sexuality are best not talked about at all. If only it would go away . . .

Clowns and nonconformists are needed for laughter and variety, but not to receive the abuse of the majority who cannot resolve their own inner conflicts. Indeed, the very structure of thought, the very rules of the game, of nonconformist, of handicapped, need to be challenged. For the message is clear to each of us who may be in some position of power: It is only from the people you are tempted to turn into outcasts that you can discover what it means to be wholly yourself – and there is certainly no discovery if there is total exclusion. Not only can we *learn* from them, we actually *need* them.

In the world as it is *now*, some of us may have to bear more than our share of this corporate disease of scapegoating from which we all suffer. That disease has afflicted severely the Jewish and Christian peoples. But I do discern the radical contribution made by Jesus himself, and fitfully glimpsed since, which overturned these diseased values. He demonstrated in his own person that however much you may try, you cannot in the end banish or kill what you loathe. At least that is what the Resurrection is all about for me.

Once you know that is true, you can give up the whole weary business of categories and scapegoats, of describing *people* in terms of an isolated limb or a supposed sexual or other defect. *Then* we can turn the phrase "you're handicapped and I want to do all I can to help you" into the response, "Maybe not as fertile, but often just as fruitful."

2
Oppression

1. THAT FILM

"The central issue of self-oppression runs like an open wound unbalmed through the film." So warned *The Observer* in its preview of the BBC film, *The Lord's my Shepherd and He Knows I'm Gay*. Were those of us who were interviewed indulging in a bout of self-oppression? Most of the letters I've received since have been complimentary ones. Honesty was the word most often used. Others were glad that the film was cool, calm, and collected. They didn't find it threatening; they were relieved. Well, I suppose that's all right from the point of view of those whose ignorance and prejudice were dented just a little. Maybe it was about as much of the unfamiliar as they could take.

So, we're honest and reasonable people, those who are gay and Christian. And bland. But then the questions. Where were the women? There was nothing in the film to demolish the myth that 'homo' in 'homosexual' means 'man'. And there were the images of lifestyles: the married gay priest, the celibate gay monk, the gay couple whose lives were sufficiently like those of a married couple not to disturb people too much (the cat on a copy of *Gay News* – discerning moggie, that – and the walk into the sunset at the end). None of this is to cast doubt on the sincerity or integrity of the people concerned, just to say that the images portrayed, powerful as always on television, were of gay men living within the frame of reference of the majority. "We're not all that much different." Now of course the individual may make the genuine choice that happens to coincide with the majority's feelings of what is comfortable: there's a rhetoric of the left that refuses to allow that such a choice could be genuine and free. But it is true that those of us who took part in the film were caught in the assumptions of the outsider looking in.

Then I scrutinized the brief appearance of one who is neither married nor celibate by vocation nor living in a permanent relationship. He talked of the way in which the experience of the gay person growing up was a useful human preparation for being ordained. How? By enabling him to cope with being in a minority (dog collars and Glad To Be Gay badges both proclaim a minority status in their different ways) and with living much of the time on his own. Now this is a subtle one. On the one hand every human being is in a minority in some way or other and has to come to terms with that fact, and it's a mark of human maturity to be able to be on your own for a long period and be content. On the other hand, I suddenly exploded to myself, Why should that lesson have to be learned *simply because you are gay*? Yes, it was all right in an interview to talk about being in a minority, but why not point out that the minority is *for no good reason* oppressed rather than valued? And why not object to the way in which the majority loads so much fear and guilt on to the gay person that it is still a great struggle to emerge from isolation and loneliness? As *The Observer* said, there wasn't much in the film to "encourage the isolated gay".

In a minor key, shouldn't priests, gay or not, stop accepting the terms of the game that places them on lonely pedestals, often proud and pale, above it all? Well, I can write that only as a priest who once disliked being knocked off such a pedestal, and who now rather enjoys climbing off it to be more human! Pity though that it takes reflection after an event to heal another of the open wounds.

II. THE OPPRESSION OF SILENCE

It was one of those wedding receptions where the man on his own is asked the inevitable question by a group of be-hatted women, "Is your wife with you?" "No," I replied, "I'm not married." "A bachelor then?" Before I could say anything further, another voice cut in, "A gay one?" There was laughter at this, but when I said calmly, "Yes, actually", the laughter became an embarrassed titter which faded into silence.

At least it was better than the kind of thing I used to reply, "Oh no, no one on the horizon yet," accompanied by the kind of smile that invites sympathy. How self-oppressed you can be – and you often don't see it until years later.

Most people find a truthful answer hard to respond to. They find themselves handling what for them is a sexual hot potato. Hence the silence. Even half-truths are sufficiently awkward to knock many people off their social perch. If I just answer a plain "No" to the question, "Are you married?", the terseness is abrupt and unexpected. If I answer, as a friend of mine does, "No, that's not my orientation," there is a puzzled silence. Both answers create a vacuum that is difficult to fill, especially if you're not prepared to say anything more.

Mind you, it's a vacuum that cries out to be filled with a *positive* statement. (Notice that the answers which start with a 'no' have all been on the questioner's terms.) A statement like this: "I'm gay. I'm happy about it, and I wish I could introduce you to the guy I live with, but he works on Saturdays." If *that's* followed by silence, at least *you've* taken the initiative. You can look round the wedding reception and say, "Have you ever thought how everything in our society favours those who get married? Like John and Mary today. Gay people are virtually ignored." Or, in lighter vein, "I think the best man's gorgeous, don't you?"

I think that silence is one of the subtlest forms of oppression, particularly that awkward silence of parents and teachers and priests over gayness. There's the silence that gives a young person no frame of reference, no words and concepts to give shape to his or her tentative feelings and experiences. It's the silence that whispers the lie about Uncle George, that he's been sacked because he – er – lost his temper with the boss. It's the silence that keeps the married couple feeling totally isolated when one of them becomes aware of his or her gay-ness, and they know no one with whom they can share the perplexities that crowd in on them. It's the silence that is the removal of descriptions of gay love from translations and second editions of stories and poems. It's the silence of those who say on the telephone, "Now about – er – this matter," or "This – er – movement you're involved with," or "Can I come and talk over a certain question – you know what I mean?"

Part of the relief of coming out is the inner decision, "I shall no longer consent to the silence that others impose on me. I shall not live my life within the boundaries that other people feel safe with. If I do on occasion keep silent, it will not be out of fear, but because I judge that it would do more harm than good were I to speak at this moment." From then on, awkward silences will nearly always be the responsibility of others. No longer are you oppressing yourself. *You* can decide how far (and increasingly it becomes, Not very far) you are willing to go along with those who say, "I don't mind what you do, as long as you keep quiet about it and I don't have to think."

There are even marvellous silences when you and an old friend, or a parent, have got over all awkwardness and embarrassment, have thoroughly talked through what your gayness means to you, and at the end are content just to be quiet together. Some of us would say that it is in that kind of reconciling silence that you particularly discern the presence of God.

III. THE MIND OF THE OPPRESSED

"I have been going round in a daze for years, simply accepting that everybody else was right in saying that I was bent and queer. I think I stopped feeling and responding. I became mouse-like and forgot I had a lion within. Heavens, I don't think I even *started* feeling and responding as the genuine me; I'd forgotten how to!"

So says the person who had begun to realize the extent of the oppression that has been such a burden for years. It's as if a heavy weight has been pressing down, squeezing out all life and feeling, making a person prickly and defensive and withdrawn, at best smiling and compliant in public. But behind the mask there's so much twisted self-hatred. It's all on a par with the falseness that Jesus was angry about: he saw the religious leaders of his day imprison others (and themselves) with burdensome regulations that effectively anaesthetized the human spirit.

Many refused even to see that these things were so. Many still refuse to open their eyes and ears. At best there's a private adjustment with one's conscience – but in public we're like everybody else. It's a desperate split, the left hand not knowing what the right hand is doing. There can be a profound *forgetting*, the spinning of an elaborate web of self-deception, a playing of games where the rules are so ancient that they don't even have to be learnt. They're simply absorbed from the cradle onwards. "If I let you see how false and hypocritical I've been, then you may not like me any more – and that's something I daren't risk." Who hasn't lived like that? We have wandered around in a grey miasma of our own unrecognized intrigue. (I gather that Steve Biko, the black leader in South Africa who died in prison, commented that there was nothing that helped the oppressor so much as the mind of the oppressed.)

The contrast could not be greater with the joy and the relief of saying NO MORE. At the very least, from this day on I'll be honest with myself. Now, at last, I've begun to *see*, nudged and prompted by the prophets and their badges that challenge and annoy. No longer will I dismiss the activists just because they're angry and I'm nice. The lion has woken up and is flexing his throat muscles. The energy begins to move; the paralysis loosens; the defensive armour begins to drop away; the fog clears. It hurts, yes, by God it hurts (and that's not swearing, it's true), layer upon layer of accumulated pain coming to the surface. But to be without feeling is to be dead. You can't be alive without feeling hurt. You recognize the choice at last – dead and safe and cocooned and numb, or alive and at risk, exposed to hurt as well as joy.

The pain and the fog don't go away all at once. Time and again a voice says, Enough for now. No more just yet. Let me rest for a bit. But once you have unleashed the spirit of truth, it will never let you go.

And this is exactly the way in which the challenge of the Christian gospel can actually strike home to you if you are gay. You can hear the good news of freedom only when you have admitted how much you are oppressed. The journey from that point on takes you a long time. There is the inner moment of change when you give up, at great cost to your comfort, the mentality and attitudes of the oppressed. There is the wilderness of your own personal pain – though you will find others there, and occasionally you will hear echoes from your own past when you hear another struggling with that moment of challenge, and you will encourage and be encouraged. There is the confrontation with the Pharaohs of this world who protect themselves from their own fear of love and freedom by exercising too much power with too little wisdom, using it to bind rather than to free. And once in a while you may know the place where the lion and the lamb lie down together, power and love reconciled, oppressor and oppressed at last giving up their game of mutual destruction and recognizing each other as fellow human beings.

3
Secrets

I. AN OPEN SECRET?

We were talking about a certain trial and the screeds of coverage in the newspapers. "Whoever you are," he said, "you can't keep your sexuality in a private compartment. One way and another, by what you think and by how you behave, and by what other people think and how they respond, the whole of your life is influenced by the ways in which you find others attractive."

The *whole* of your life? I wondered if that was true, say, for the closeted. True for the person who keeps very hidden, lives a very secretive sex life? Yes, in fact we have no choice in this matter. Like it or not, our sexuality *is* thoroughly mixed in with the rest of our lives. The one affects the other and we can't avoid it. We might like to *pretend* that we can live in compartments ("My sexuality is my own business," we hear it said, "it's my private life, and it has nothing to do with anyone else"), but life just doesn't work out like that – even if we're trying to live at the extreme of secrecy. For a start, our sexuality then becomes the dominant, if hidden, theme of our lives. It's our master not our servant. It's the theme of our fantasies, dreams and thoughts. It exercises a power and a fascination over us. It controls us but isn't an integrated part of us. We live according to the rules of the society around us, according to the desires of most people who want us to hide it all away. The rest of our lives *is* affected. Sex cannot be just an individual and private matter.

Then there are those who are almost secret and know only hidden, often anonymous sex, in the dark. It's not fulfilling because only a bit of the person is involved. The hunt for the next, supposedly better encounter, is never far away. It's a vicious circle precisely because it's a secret one. Again a person plays along with the rules, society's rules, the rules of others. "No one must know who I am, even my sexual partner." "If someone does find out – and I hope that I haven't been recognized – then of course I accept that I must suffer according to the rules as I've absorbed them."

It's only when you don't mind who knows you're gay that you can allow your sexuality and the rest of your life and personality to have the chance to relate harmoniously. The sexually alive and honest person is far from being the mechanical bed-hopper, but is vibrant and sensual in every situation, with lots of energy and always the possibility of love. You may or may not be living in a relationship that is somewhat akin to a childless marriage – you may even be celibate – but neither you nor anyone else (at least those who aren't secret about *their* sexuality – and unfortunately that's most people some of the time) will be able to pretend that you're a non-sexual being. You don't actually have to say anything or display anything (or even have your name in *Gay News*!). You'll be warm and affectionate, fully alive with both sexes, recognizing that sexual attraction is playing a large part in your relationships, giving them a ground-base, as it were, from which to grow. Whenever you're like this, touch taboos crumble, and it is very good indeed just to be close.

Dare I say, without being open to misunderstanding, that Jesus was like this? In the sense that no human being can avoid the challenge of integrating his or her sexuality with the rest of living? A man who was completely loving must have done that. It was part of the *aliveness* that made the fearful cower and then attack him.

The secretive can never understand that such loving knows from inside how to behave with care and respect; it doesn't need detailed rules of behaviour in advance. The secretive in fact live by strict, often harsh rules. They're dominated by them, either of their own or others' making. "Don't show affection in public." "Don't give any clue away that you find others of your own sex attractive." "Live by society's expectations: you'll get on that way." Once you've realized what that does to you, you realize what a weight and burden it all is. And some crack out of the loneliness it brings.

The life and freedom that Jesus lived was just too much for most people. In the end it left him in a minority of one. To live in a zone of freedom is to be vulnerable to attack by the imprisoned outside the zone. Strange reversal! Those who think they're free cannot even hear the clanking of their own chains. They've forgotten that they've chosen comfort and death rather than risk and life. But they remember enough to rise up in wrath against anyone who's different and dares to disturb their slumber.

Thank God that such life and freedom and loving does happen among us. Thank God that when it's fully expressed it can never be extinguished. It's irrepressible. It even bounces back from the death-dealing blows that the frightened powerful deal out. No wonder that those who've perceived the clue, who've begun to live this way, want to celebrate a *birth* at Christmas.

II. LAMBDAS

Driving along a Hertfordshire road recently, I was overtaken by a car displaying a Greek letter 'L' – a lambda – in the back window. I was intrigued – and then amused to discover that the driver was the Administrative Secretary of the Gay Christian Movement.

For some people the lambda is a kind of code, a secret sign of recognition, the badge of an underground movement in a hostile world – like the fish scrawled by the early Christians on the walls of the catacombs of Rome. For others, it is too well known for that: it's dangerous to wear, for they fear that they might be recognized in the wrong places. For others again, there's the hope that they *will* be recognized, and they are glad to say what the sign means – and risk being bumped by a following car! (It was a *very* large lambda, not a discreet lapel badge).

Some gay people, often of an older generation, resent the great secret cover being blown. They struggled to find a way of surviving in a society that labelled them criminal and sinful. It had taken a certain granite courage to carve out at least a part of life that said, This territory is mine, and I admit no intruders. Rightly or wrongly, public knowledge would have been anticipated as disaster and obliteration, disgrace and exile. Sheer survival depended on secrecy.

Not that this was necessarily a matter of keeping the secret to yourself: many did 'come out' at least to themselves and to a few others. The trouble was that the public secrecy, together with the public prejudice and fear, had the result of too many people in fact refusing to recognize themselves. Even now some people blame the Devil (or their parents or society) for their furtive and secret encounters of anonymous sex, when even the face of the other is not seen. And *that* kind of secret becomes an incredible burden. Also it encourages a lack of responsibility for yourself and your relationships, a lack of trust and self-respect.

Even for those who built their relationships in the ghetto, there were those dangers on a wider scale, that of their connection with the rest of society. Or, by compensation, there grew a distorted sense of superiority over the rest of the world.

Today the lambda can be a sign of an open secret, not a closed one. An open secret is still something of a mystery to the onlooker, for it can be thoroughly known only from the inside. But at least there can be communication. The open secret can be known about, talked about, recognized. And in fact one's sense of identity is clarified and deepened in the process – it isn't taken away as the closeted fear.

Indeed, there may grow a sense, not of superiority, but of being privileged people with a great deal to offer to others. E.M. Forster wrote in *What I Believe*: "I believe in aristocracy . . . Not an aristocracy of power, based on rank and influence, but an aristocracy of the sensitive, the considerate, and the plucky. Its members are found in all nations and classes and through all the ages, and there is a secret understanding between them when they meet. They represent the true human tradition, the one queer victory over cruelty and chaos."

Of course there are personal steps in declaring an open secret. A partial coming out among other gays can build up a sense of positive identity and self-confidence, and that can be a necessary time of secrecy from, say, parents, until you feel good enough about yourself to be positive about telling them.

Even when you have come out in the sense of being glad for anyone to know that you're gay, there will still be secrets that are perfectly valid, secrets that should be shared only with a few. For the deepest bonds between human beings are forged among close friends. I need time to build up trust enough to tell my life-story. All manner of difficulties get in the way of that, and a public coming out doesn't automatically solve them!

Further, there is the secret unique journey of every human being. We cannot be defined and limited by definitions of our sexuality. We are indeed sexual creatures, but much more. Our gayness should connect with other parts of our lives and personalities, affecting them and being affected by them, and the quest for the meaning of that sexuality will involve asking how it can benefit the whole community. (Indeed, the word 'gay' may best be used in this sense of making the connections: it is much more than a sexual attraction.) And yet the question, Who am I?, can never be completely answered in sexual or personal or societal terms. There is a spiritual quest too, bound up with sexuality and society, yes, but having its own uniqueness. There is a marvellous sentence in the strangest of books in the New Testament, the Revelation to John, that says of the person who is "victorious", that "I will give him a white stone" (symbol of integrity and wholeness) "with a new name written on the stone, known only to the one who receives it."

III. COURAGE

"I cannot demand courage of anyone: I can but applaud it when I see it." That was said to me when I was beginning to come out and say that I was gay. The trouble is that courage needs daily exercise – most of us are lucky if we manage it once a week. Even if you've come out, you need courage not least to stay out, and not retreat back into a cosy but fearful closet whose doormat says 'quiet desperation'.

A priest wrote that to be courageous is to "believe that there is more to be done with life than prolong it". Anxiety and fear keep us in prolonged traps where nothing changes: a grey half-life goes on and on. We 'hang on' (with hang-ups?) to some substitute for living, be it possessions or a safe style of relating to others. We fear being laughed at or losing our job. We build up carefully manicured and cosmetic façades.

But those who try and hang on to life will lose it – those who let go will find it. And that's always true, not least when you're tempted by a voice that says, No more, you've been courageous enough, time to relax for a while: you've had enough of being battered for who you really are.

If you have much to do with the Church, the message will be, Be cautious. It then takes courage to be bold. If you're something as outrageously old-fashioned as a preacher, you find your hands tied: it's hard to be prophetic at a family service. After all, some things aren't suitable for children. I liked Dame Edna Everidge's question to a 12-year-old boy who came on to the stage at the end of the show: Did you find it suitable this evening? Subtle chains surround taboos, and it needs courage to dare to break them. Dame Edna does it. Lenny Bruce did it.

It needs courage to say what you feel (not what you *ought* to say — by the current dogma of Gay Lib or the C of E). Courage to be honest and clear — not to pretend and say, I love you, when you really mean, I fancy you. Courage not to shift responsibility on the the other and ask, When are you coming round again? Harder to make an honest statement which leaves the other free: I want to see you again soon very much indeed.

It needs courage to talk to the scared unattractive character and know how to give of yourself without raising his hopes that he's found his Prince Charming at last.

It takes courage to *ask* for what you need — that might be to be held silently in another's arms for half an hour. Somehow you think you ought to be more sexy. It's sometimes harder to ask for affection than for sex. (Correspondingly, some people avoid sex and close relationships by saying, I want to be warm and affectionate with everyone.)

It may even take courage to make friends with the opposite sex (yes, warm and affectionate) and risk being thought by your friends to be heterosexual.

It takes courage to go to a disco alone, risking sending out the message, I'm lonely — especially if you're not yet proud of those grey flecks of hair or those creeping lines across the face.

I suppose courage means that you're no longer bothered about yourself or about what other people think of you. It's a total lack of self-concern. It's living the present moment with the whole of you, and taking no anxious thought for tomorrow. If today is lived well, that's storing up plenty of fuel for tomorrow's being lived even better.

It may have something to do with compassion as well. "Where there is no courage," to quote the priest again, "compassion dwindles, and where compassion is absent courage tends to become arrogant self-display."

IV. THE COTTAGE AND THE CONFESSIONAL

Come on, now, you must be joking. You can't put the unmentionable and the sacred side by side like that . . . What, two sides of the same coin? . . . Both part of a guilt-trap?

Consider. A nineteenth-century Roman Catholic or High Anglican church, probably in neo-gothic style. In a side aisle you'll notice a series of confessionals – boxes with two compartments, one for priest and one for penitent. You go in and shut the door, and you are aware that there is someone in the adjacent compartment. It's all very private; it needs to be. But it may also be anonymous – neither person may know the name of the other.

I suppose it's fanciful to compare this with other adjacent cubicles in those small buildings often to be found by the entrance to parks and market places? The similarities are uncanny when you start to think about it.

Secret stories are told in both places – spoken in the case of one, scribbled on walls in the case of the other. And there is a sort of communication going on, though it tends to be impersonal. Vulnerable secrets are told or vulnerable parts are put forward – in the hope that they will be accepted, received, affirmed. Above all there must be no rejection.

Many come to both out of loneliness and guilt, believing themselves to be unacceptable. They find something, often only temporary relief, no more. It can all be very mechanical and partial – a list of misdeeds, the tip of yourself. A Roman Catholic writer, Sebastian Moore, referred to confession once as a 'private appointment with guilt'. It could be a description of the other encounter too.

Nothing is ever said about these meetings afterwards. If one should happen to recognize the other in the street, there is no acknowledgment. The secret is well kept. You certainly never refer to the detail of what happened or what was said and done. Lips are sealed.

If that were the whole truth of sex and religion, we would be in a sorry state. But an institution that has often driven sex underground can hardly be surprised if it sometimes surfaces in the shadows in a way that imitates and mocks and judges.

Whatever is secret and in the dark must come into the light of day, to be known and understood and made whole with the rest of our personality. Of course the details of one's personal life are private and never to be shared with more than one or two well-chosen people. But the sharing is best when it's face to face.

There's something destructive about a pattern of life that is dominated by only one way of sexual relating and only one kind of religious practice. The mechanics of rituals, both words and deeds, need to be filled out with personal meaning if they are not to become meaningless yet compulsive repetitions.

But one good thing has been happening these past years. The need for affirmation *is* being sought and met face to face. Both spiritual and sexual growth can happen only in relationship, not in the kind of secrecy where one refuses to be known. And both kinds of growth demand courage.

It is surely no coincidence that more secrets are told in bed than anywhere else. The atmosphere is one of trust and acceptance and you can dare to say something about that side of yourself that you usually keep hidden – the guilty, the fearful, the stupid.

It's the same in a counselling relationship, or one with a sprititual guide or 'soul-friend'. You know that here, if nowhere else, you can say anything, and the other respectfully and caringly 'receives' all that is said. You will be accepted and affirmed.

In these ways our past hurts are healed. There is more of God in them than in many an empty ritual. Anything that is said or done in a ritual way in a church can but focus and deepen the truth of what is being lived out elsewhere.

Anonymous sex and the reeling off of habitual sins are of course easier – they dodge the painful bits of you. Avoiding the cost is ungodly ease, and in fact leads to the worse pain of deepening despair.

How often is the cry heard, What I really want is friendship . . . It is unlikely that it will start when two people meet and each of them is in a mood of compulsive ritual, whether that be sexual or religious in context. I think it's true that both styles have begun to crumble, though of course there's more to be said about each than these analogies suggest. And come to think of it, you don't hear shouts of joy or sighs of peace when only the formulae and the motions have been gone through – in cottage or confessional.

4
Comment

I. I REFUSE MY CONSENT

A visit to Auschwitz isn't everybody's idea of a holiday excursion. But it's a haunting place and you can't forget it once you've seen it. Thank God it's a museum today, and not a prison camp. It's in Poland, that vulnerable buffer country between Germany and Russia. For the Poles the memory is still vivid of the Nazi occupation and of the results of one kind of political extremism. For obvious reasons, today's unease is muted about the Gulag Archipelago of the other political extreme.

Having recently seen this starkest of museums, I think I'm right in saying that gay people aren't specifically mentioned among the victims of the gas chambers. There is merely an inscription to those imprisoned for political and social reasons. But there is a pink triangular badge among the flowers by the simple memorial urn of ashes – in the barracks where one grey wall is now given over to the awful words, "Four million people died here."

Why did it happen? I've been used to laying 100% of the blame at the door of Hitler's mad racial idealism; I've regarded the Jewish people as totally innocent, an obvious target for frustrations and hatreds. But how was it that so many of those people were deceived, millions – meekly it seems – going to their deaths? Who kept silent in the thirties? Who refused to step across boundaries – both ways – and make friends, and so weave a mesh that no dictator would have been able to undo? Were there no effective protests at the beginning of it all? Or were people too concerned, as they still are, with private life – and so just didn't see? In some mysterious way, were *both* sides caught up in a mutual blindness, gripped by the terrible illusion that 'we' can survive only at 'their' expense? Are there never enough people to stand up and say, I refuse my consent to this? For silence gives consent.

An angry young man in Trevor Griffiths' play, *Comedians*, shouts: "The Jews stayed in line, even when they *knew*. What's *that* about? I stand in no line. I refuse my consent."

Yet the historical point was reached when the individual was powerless to effect change. So came the day of the mass victim, destroyed at the turn of a gas tap, utterly without power. And that now is the threat not only to gay people when the forces of ignorance and fear and prejudice are stirred, but to all of us under the threat of the mushroom cloud. The game of oppressor and victim can no longer be played: the stakes are too high. Never was the need greater for gay people to come out and say to education authorities, medical authorities, politicians, bishops: I refuse my consent. With the young man in the play, Gethen Price, we cry 'NO' to Auschwitz, a No in anger against mass cruelty and murder. We must refuse our consent – and at the same time not turn the game of oppressor and victim on its head, reversing a coin of hatred and creating other Auschwitzes.

The dramatic tension in the play lies between the attitude of Price and that of his tutor, Waters. Price is training to be a comedian and performs a cabaret turn that is very funny but icy, cold, hateful of human beings. Afterwards Waters retorts, "No compassion, no truth. You threw it all out. Love, care, concern, call it what you like, you junked it over the side."

It's a knife edge. It's an almost impossible demand. To fight for justice and freedom without losing compassion and without becoming soft. It's the difficulty of seeing that even Camp Commandant Hoess was not a totally evil man – AND it's the difficulty of seeing that the Jewish people had their share of responsibility. For to be pushed into and to accept the safety of the ghetto is actually to increase fear and the possibility of murder, to accept the role of scapegoat and victim. On *both* sides we are talking of ordinary people often enough, of clerks and guards and teachers and drivers who loved their families and friends and played Beethoven on their pianos. In the play, Waters talks to Price about his visit to Buchenwald at the end of the war. He realized that in essence it was not a unique place, just one horrific example of what happens when hatred reigns. The difference is only one of scale and degree between Auschwitz and a father's twisted contempt for his gay son or daughter. As Waters comments, "We've gotta get deeper than hate. Hate's no help."

Hitler's is not the 'final solution', however tempted we are to want the annihilation of others. There is a different solution: to forgive and be forgiven. Yet our power to forgive, our desire to, our ability to, is limited. We still want revenge for pains inflicted on us, glad to find a group of people, or even one other, willing to be our scapegoat. It's a costly business, forgiveness, this final but creative solution. It's hard enough on the personal level, let alone the international. Out of the ashes of Auschwitz, however, comes the stark alternative: annihilation or forgiveness. It's the challenge of the mind of Christ who saw into the heart of both pharisee and prostitute. It works by deepening the conviction of a Polish mystic of the seventeenth century who was born in Silesia, not all that far from Auschwitz: that though the cost may be life itself,

> There is no higher aim
> than to reclaim
> another, blinded by life's pain,
> to help him see and live again.

II. AN OPEN LETTER

To the Rt Revd John Baker, Bishop of Salisbury.

Dear Bishop,

I enjoyed reading your article, *The Christian, sexuality, and AIDS* in the magazine *Christian* – the issue for September/ October 1987. You write as someone with a deep respect for tradition yet open to fresh thinking. I found myself agreeing with most of what you said, but puzzled when you wrote this: "Our bodies as they have evolved within God's creation, are clearly made for heterosexual intercourse. If we are to become beings integrated in body, mind, heart and spirit, our sexual orientation needs to conform to this physical datum." This seems to me to interpret nature in a static way, not far from the blueprint theory of creation in which everything is completely given at the beginning with no room for the unexpected or the creatively new. I would wish to argue that an evolving creation is in the process of becoming more varied and complex. On a static view you might well argue that mouths were 'made' for biting, tearing, and chewing food, and that penises, anuses, and vaginas were 'made' for eliminating waste products. Clearly, penises and vaginas have always been used for reproduction, but who first got the idea that the act of intercourse might be prolonged beyond the few moments necessary for ejaculation? Who first discovered that mouths could be used for the pleasures of kissing as well as for masticating? After all, kissing isn't necessary for survival.

Again, someone first discovered that the organs of the mouth could be used for something more varied and complex than mere sounds. Gradually we moved from the grunts of our ancestors to the Gielguds of the English language. Speaking Shakespeare mellifluously is not necessary for survival.

So it seems to me that it is entirely natural that human beings should explore a variety of ways of sexual contact. In this understanding, same-sex relationships are a variant which does not necessarily lead to disintegration and disharmony.

If sex is about quality of relationship and therefore about nurture, healing, and pleasure, then we can move beyond the need to 'conform' to a 'physical datum', beyond what looks like a determinist view of biology and a confusion of the primary biological function of reproduction with the primary personal function of maturing in relationship. Otherwise, we are in danger of judging the violent thrusting of rape as slightly less sinful than an act of sexual intercourse between two people of the same sex who love each other deeply.

I can understand the argument that claims that an ecstasy of union is likely to be achieved supremely in an act of heterosexual intercourse, because the flow of two bodies in wave-like motion is technically more easily sustainable in this way than in any other. But degrees of ecstasy add nothing to the moral argument, and I would suggest that for most people trust, humour, playfulness, and passionate and relaxed touch are more likely than anything else sexual to give intimations of blissful, non-possessive love, flourishing by enabling the other to flourish, mutually. Is not this the chastity that is the goal of all our loving?

You write that 'natural' refers to the 'use and fulfilment of creation in the way God intends.' I am not sure if that is the way the word 'natural' is usually understood and used, but I certainly go along with the importance of being attuned to what God intends, though I would want to say 'ways' rather than 'way', for we must surely allow for what is new in creation. I can agree that this will need to be consonant with the revelation we have received about the life of heaven, of eternal life, of creation transfigured. At its heart will be that flourishing which we experience in and through those acts of enabling others to flourish, in which we discover our deepest pleasure and delight. It would be the claim of many gay people that their intimate sexual loving has enabled them to glimpse that life.

III. WE SHALL REMEMBER THEM

The pomp and circumstance of Remembrance Sunday appears more ridiculous every year. Why remember events that happened before half of us were born? But underneath the ceremonial and the singing at the Cenotaph and the Royal

Albert Hall are thousands of *particular* memories and *particular* stories, from the old woman in her bedsit with the faded photograph of a fiancé killed in the Battle of the Somme to a recent book published that we might know more of the truth of the events of the bombing of Hiroshima. It is these that are important to remember, not with an apathetic shrug, but acknowledging that offences against the human spirit were committed by both sides in the world wars, that individuals and their memories and concerns are important, that there is a need for symbolic moments to renew determination to work at removing the causes of war.

All of which is preliminary and a kind of parable. I now have in mind the tomb of the Unknown Warrior in Westminster Abbey, a symbol of those who have no grave and no named headstone. There is not even that inadequate memorial for those who were killed because they were gay – like the thousands in Hitler's concentration camps. Even where there is a memorial, most of the world would have us forget that some of its heroes were gay – including the poet of the First World War, Wilfrid Owen, some of whose poems were not published until Jon Stallworthy's biography appeared. And I don't recall ever having seen a grave shared by two lovers of the same sex. Even the occasional memorial tablet in a church is muted. "In gratitude and in loving memory: to a loyal friend": that has to serve as a way of keeping particular memories alive. It can do so only for as long as the partner survives: another death, and there is no way of celebrating and remembering the love that was between them.

Another side to this 'forgetting' is the lonely grief of those who have loved and been bereaved, and have been unable to share that grief. There has been nobody around whom they can trust enough. And because the relationship and the gayness were so much tied in with the whole life of the one who had died, the surviving partner is tongue-tied even when asked kindly how things are by family and neighbours. There is nobody with whom memories can be 'grieved through'.

Gradually others forget the past: yet another story has no record to enable it to become part of everyone's shared inheritance. We all become losers.

Obviously any act of remembrance cannot be artificially devised. To be symbolic it must arise spontaneously out of events that happen. I'm glad that the Gay Christian Movement has decided to start a Michael Harding Memorial Address, prompted though it has been by a tragedy. Michael was killed in a road accident in February, dying out of due time in his mid-twenties, just as he'd begun to be open as a gay priest and work actively for gay people. Many of his friends want something tangible, symbolic, to 'remember' him by – not in any morbid wallowing, but as a way of recalling his story and his presence, and so in turn to give a little more meaning to the stories of others, the details of which will forever remain silent.

And there is more to it than that. Remembrance Sunday becomes a mockery if it dwells on the past, especially if it exaggerates the glory and forgets the horror. It needs by its ritual to move us to work for peace. So on any anniversaries of special significance to gay people, there needs to be renewed that determination to be rid of those barriers that would bury the stories and memories of so many people in the silence of the grave.

IV. ONWARD GAY CHRISTIAN SOLDIERS

When my doctor thinks my health can stand it, he lets me have a look at the *Daily Telegraph*. (Mind you, I thought I was ready for anything after seeing a Gay Pride '79 badge on Debbie's lapel in a pub in a remote village in Devon – you just can't get away from them these days, they're everywhere). But it *was* a bit of a shock to read a proposal in the *Telegraph* for a gay élite corps in the army. Was this England or Ancient Greece?

". . . the Armed Forces, while retaining their existing ban on homosexual behaviour for most of their personnel, should deliberately recruit special units of homosexuals to whom a different kind of disciplinary code would apply. Such bodies would at first no doubt be the victims of mockery but in the long run could they not actually become élite units?"

So suggests Christie Davies, senior lecturer in sociology at Reading University. Well, is this why the Territorial Army is being strengthened? Not against the day of civil strife, but because the Regular (or is it Ir-regular) Army can't cope with the flood of applicants referred to them by Gay Switchboard, Friend, and Icebreakers? What was that whisper about the Gay Gordons Regiment?

But wait. Not only the Army – the Church as well. But this is perhaps reading far too much into the suggestion that the Church need not any longer "impose sanctions on homosexuals simply in order to preserve internal discipline." The two bastions of male dominance crumbling? A turnabout by the Church of England – you can't be a bishop unless you're gay? We weren't expecting *that* from the long-awaited report. Perhaps Christie Davies has some inside information? But of course – a moment's thought and you realize that you're on the wrong tack. If the Church had an élite, it couldn't possibly be a gay one. Elites are always small, and there are just too many gay clergy around for them to be able to form one. You'd have a job getting all of them into either of the two cathedrals that face each other across the Thames.

The old institutions must be desperate about their survival if the advocates of a rigid *status quo* are reduced to farce. But the article is useful if only to show the logic of a certain kind of tolerance.

Allow small exceptions to the rules and the rules will actually be strengthened – this is the general line. Encourage gay relationships that are modelled on marriage, and you will strengthen the institution of marriage as we know it. It's like introducing a bit of group therapy into a hospital without allowing it to put fundamental questions to the arrangement whereby 'patients' and 'staff' are trapped in roles of ignorance and dependency on the one side and expertise and dominance on the other, all within a hierarchial order with its minutely negotiated grades of pay. There are usually too many people with a vested interest in not allowing such experiments to succeed: most of us most of the time prefer comfort and familiarity.

So Christie Davies writes: "Our main aim should be to provide fair play and decent treatment for those men unfortunate enough to be homosexual" (What? No women in the army?) "in such a way as to buttress rather than dismember our existing institutions."

The article traces our sexual taboos to the ancient Israelites, who thought it essential to maintain a sharp boundary between "God's chosen people and the idolatrous heathen". To do this they had to keep the boundary between male and female clear. The taboo is hardly questioned: "Church and military leaders see homosexuals as breaking down the division between male and female, and thus threatening the separateness and distinctive prestige of their organizations. . . A brigadier might take up with a corporal or a bishop with a curate."

Such notions of institutional life, with a supposedly necessary hierarchy, separateness, classification – they influence us all. But we might at least question this way of arranging our community life. In fact, we've often lost sight of the notion of community at all. We hand over responsibility quite inappropriately to others when we could easily take it on ourselves. Leaders and experts forget that it's their job to serve others, to learn about them, and to enable them to do things for themselves. To be put into an élite is just another way of creating a ghetto. People still miss each other. Better to admit that old ways are crumbling and to crumble a bit with them – and allow ourselves to take new shape. Dying to live is one of the names of the game.

V. WHO OFFENDS?

A man joins his local amateur dramatic society. He's 28, and very welcome because the society is always short of male actors. He's likeable and soon becomes popular with the other members. A number of youngsters help behind the scenes, and there's a flourishing young people's section.

Over the months a friendship grows between him and a ten-year-old boy. It's all open and easy and good. The man is a frequent visitor in the boy's home, and is accepted and liked by the boy's mother and father.

Some three or four or maybe five years later, somebody talks to the director of the society (or is it the vicar responsible for the church hall where the society meets, or to the boy's head teacher?). He says he's worried: he's sure there's something "unhealthy" about this relationship. Nothing much is said of course. Indeed it hadn't occurred to anybody until now to ask any questions. But a watch is kept, and anxieties grow.

"Yes, I hadn't noticed just how much time they spend together. And I didn't know they go walking in the country together in the summer. It's against the law, isn't it? I've a friend in the local police force: I'll ask his advice."

Watching, observing – or is it spying? No one counts the working hours involved for the police – at our expense. One day, the police, hidden near a footpath miles away from the town where they live, suddenly pounce – caught red-handed with an adult arm round a young shoulder. An immediate arrest.

There's a charge brought, and a court case to come. The police frighten the boy with their questions – at the boy's home, when the mother and father are out. He admits to anything they suggest. The man pleads guilty. He's persuaded to. He's told it will protect his friend from being dragged through the courts. The local press have a field day – rumours, distortions, exaggerations, the whole ghastly language of monsters and victims. Within days – hours almost – the

whole town knows who the two are: so much for protection
from the courts!

Confusion reigns among the boys in the drama society.
They're interested, excited, puzzled, and hurt – someone they
all liked has suddenly disappeared, and no one will tell them
why. Some odd sayings fly around – he took a bent leap at him.
Not one adult, neither director, nor vicar, nor teacher, nor any
of the parents will take responsibility for talking to them
calmly in a language they can understand. No one can cope.
"We don't talk about that sort of thing . . . You don't
understand, you're too young."

In the end, nobody knows the truth any more. Myths sink
into the community mind. Taking advantage of the
innocent. . . For all the outsider knows, nothing illegal may
have happened at all. No one knows the truth any more – and
if they do, they're not saying. Silence descends. Another
skeleton is jammed into an already more than full cupboard.

For once, leave on one side questions of law and morals. Just
ask this: Who is innocent? Who causes damage? Whose is the
greatest offence? And don't suppose such things don't happen:
they do, even if this particular story is not factual reporting.
You see, the message gets across that it's too dangerous to
make close friends. You mustn't be seen in the company of
those much older or younger than yourself – at least not often
enough to be noticed. Who then offends? Jesus said that it
would be better if a great stone were put round your neck and
you were drowned in the sea rather than offend the young.

Yes, but who offends?

5
Can the pilot see?

(Over the past decade Pilot and True Freedom Trust, two evangelical 'counselling' services based in Poole and Merseyside respectively, have offered an approach to same-sex relationships about which I have grave misgivings. This article offers a critique of their approach.)

A rabbi told a story about a performing mouse. Its owner would put the mouse on a table and tell it to jump. To the delight of the audience the mouse would proceed to jump two feet across the table. Just to show it wasn't a fluke, the mouse would be ordered to jump again – which it would do. Then the owner would smear some glue on its feet and put it down on the table again. The order came: Jump. And the mouse wouldn't move. "Goes to show," he said, "put glue on their feet, and mice go deaf."

Our attitudes to gayness largely depend on what we see, or rather what we are willing to see, and on how we interpret what we see. If your sources are stories of scandals, of court cases, of attacks on children, of aversion therapy, then you will see one thing. If your sole sources are texts from the Bible, you're likely to make the equation, gayness=sodomy=sin, with the consequent advice: Be converted. That is what emerges from a look at the writings of O. R. Johnston of the Festival of Light* and of Pilot, the 'counselling' service on whose Council of Reference he sits. O. R. Johnston wrote in *'News Extra'*, an inset for parish magazines, "The actual practice of homosexuality, i.e. anal intercourse between men, is sinful." 'Jef' of Pilot wrote in a letter: "You know, I think that I'm going out on a limb in the near future, by declaring that there are no such things as homosexuals. Only homosexual acts." That is their

---

*I would now (1988) wish to substitute the Revd. T. Higton and the Association for Biblical Witness to our Nation.

stance, that is what they see, and that is how they interpret what they see.

The first thing to notice is that they assume that homosexual behaviour is exclusively a male preserve. It must be, of course, if sodomy is all that you see. There is an odd reluctance to mention sexual acts between women, let alone in the context of a loving relationship. But it's bound to be hard to admit the lesbian experience into your thinking if you consider that the only permissible sexual acts take place within a patriarchal family, with the man dominant over the woman. In *Homosexuality. . . an evangelical viewpoint* Jef mentions women once: ". . . any Christian woman who is subject to periodic lesbian temptations could do worse than have a medical check-up. An endocrinologist might find a hormonal imbalance." Again, it all depends on what you *see*. A Roman Catholic psychiatrist admitted at a seminar after some close questioning that his view of homosexuality as a sickness was almost entirely based on what his patients had shared with him. Further, if the only feature of gayness that you admit is anal intercourse, then you can't even begin to comment on the many other and more frequent forms of body contact between those of the same sex.

Here's a different angle of vision. Any sexual act *can*, in certain circumstances, be solely an act of domination over another person: naked force, if you like. There are four aspects of this: first, there is the aspect of conquest, the attitude of "I've got you where I want you: you're in my power." This is sadism. In the ancient near east sodomy was a sign of conquest in war (it has parallels in modern prisons), the final act of humiliating the vanquished. Second, there is the aspect of prostitution and fornication, the attitude of "I want sex now, and I don't care if you're in the mood or not. I'm using you as an object for my own pleasure." This is prostitution if paid for, fornication if not. With violence, it is rape. Third, there is the aspect of idolatry, the attitude of "You're perfect and you can give me everything I want." This is a power game if ever there was one.

At a deeper level, idolatry is the giving of *ultimate* loyalty to something or someone created rather than to the Creator. It may be that 'cultic sodomy' was bound up with this kind of idolatry in ancient times, giving homosexual acts a bad name among the Israelites. Fourth, there is the aspect of compulsion, where a life has become dominated by the power of sex, the attitude of "Sex, sex, I don't think of anything else from morning to night." I suspect that this is something else that is part of the limited vision of Pilot, for we read the testimony of one who had been for many years now "kept by Christ from the power and dominion of these sinful thoughts, desires, feelings, and affections, from which I could not, try as I would, escape for scarcely an hour in my former life." Some people see, therefore, 'excess' as the only truth about gayness. So Galileo's critics could see only what they were determined to see through his telescope.

Mind you, the more gay people come out, the less excuse there is for such blindness. Unfortunately, it is often the experience of those on the receiving end of well-meant ministrations of fundamentalists that they receive acceptance if they admit that they are wicked, but anger and cruelty if they but give the hint that they are glad – or even becoming glad – to be gay. The filter continues to work. The man is just not seen who has become more relaxed and outgoing, less arrogant and abrasive, because his personal life has become centred on another of his own sex with whom he is now living. Nor can the witness be heard of the two who realized that their sexual loving wasn't a matter of one dominating the other but rather "the two of us acting together and liking what we found" – let alone the witness of the man who came to the quiet understanding that you can live in love with another person and with God, even that God can be loved "within and as the bedrock" of that human love. There's nothing spectacular about this; nor was there about the two women who were filled with gladness and relief when they found someone willing to witness the special things they wanted to say to each other and to pray that they might be richly blessed.

The horror is that those who have not heard and seen these things, who don't yet know how to cope with their sexual feelings, the isolated and despairing, full of irrational guilt, feed the impressions of the 'helpers' that everything about gayness is bad. It's a very vicious circle. It is not helped by those who cannot *listen* to men and women who have accepted themselves as gay. Of course if they did so listen, the Jefs of this world would have to alter a good deal of their understanding of the ways of life and of God, as well as of sexuality.

On a tape that Jef made for church groups, he gives his hearers the impression that all gay people are like three of his callers: a gloomy transvestite, a married man who has fallen in love with his son-in-law, a man just out of prison. Now you would have thought that anyone offering a counselling service would spend a lot of time just listening, and then helping such people through the complexities and subtleties of their situations. Granted that no counsellor can help communicating something of his own values and attitudes, he would still be very cautious about giving advice. But that is precisely what Jef does, and fairly soon, over the telephone and in interviews. (He claims to have had conversations with 1200 callers in a year: if you know anything at all about helping people in need, the red warning light should go on there – how can you possibly be alert and sensitive to that number of people?) It seems as if the attitude is: "I know what's good for you, I don't need to listen."

I wish at least that he had the honesty to call Pilot an evangelical mission to convert non-Christian homosexuals from compulsive or trivializing sex, or, rather, in his terms, to convert sodomites to Jesus Christ, guiding them if possible to marriage and supporting them in a celibate way of life if that is not possible. Let us at least know what he is about. "With these people (i.e. the 90% of his callers who have no church background) I don't believe in non-directive counselling."

Fair enough if you're clear about it, though I would not myself be drawn to someone who said that "we often have a conversation about spiritual things – well, it's not really a conversation is it, seeing I'm doing all the talking?" What I do think is dangerous is to seem to imply that deliverance from sin = a radical change in sexual life, in orientation, desires, and actions – though he does admit that some have to bear a continuing 'burden': "After conversion, the Lord allows the homosexual condition to linger on." But that is all right by him: it is only homosexual *acts* that are sinful, "perverted eroticism corroding and spoiling the relationship."

Look at that language of corrosion for a minute. I mentioned that one of Jef's clients had been a man recently released from prison. After he'd gone, Jef says he "felt moral corruption in the atmosphere" and that he nearly broke the cup the man had been drinking from. He says he did break up the biscuits and throw them to the birds. Now I'm not denying the reality of evil atmospheres, though what causes them is a pertinent question, as is this: Is there anything within the counsellor, especially anything sexual, that he can't face and that he's projecting on to the world outside? A woman has claimed to me that Jef tried to exorcise her in the middle of a conversation, apparently without any warning or preparation. Clearly he believes that at least some gay people are possessed by an evil spirit and need deliverance from possession. It's all part of an assumed framework of belief. But wait a moment. I'm becoming familiar with a sequence of events that makes me cast grave doubts on that framework as well as on the wisdom of Jef's methods. Under the guidance of people like Jef, the person on the receiving end comes to the point of saying something like this: "Help, Lord, I'm a sinful sodomite, a degenerate, worthless creature, indulging in great wickedness." He then gives himself quite sincerely to the Lord (and I doubt nobody's sincerity in all this), and often experiences a great relief and release. "Thank you, Lord, for converting me and delivering me from this sin." If his sexual behaviour has been totally compulsive, and if he has never been able to appreciate that even in the briefest encounters there is a relief of loneliness and a stumbling towards affection, then this deliverance may be real and lasting. But even if this is so, there is no guarantee that he will not fall in love with another man, nor that he will never experience sexual desire again. If the latter is true, then something awful has indeed happened, a kind of spiritual leucotomy or castration, a removal of sexual energy. This may of course be the logic of the position of O. R. Johnston and Jef, since the former sees a kind of moral 'plague' spreading that must be stopped – but at what cost? Actual castration? It has been suggested before, not by him, but by others who share his framework of ideas. (Surely the goal is not to remove the desires but to transform them to creative and loving ends.) Here's a quotation from *The Truth in Love* (published by the Nationwide Festival of Light in 1975, of which O. R. Johnston is a leading figure). It is an assertion that is in fact dubious, but think of its implications: "The behavioural scientists now have at their disposal corrective methods which can help many." (p. 11). That sounds to me like punishment, not therapy.

Conversion, however, does not usually have that extreme effect of removing a person's sexual desires. Enforced castration might; aversion therapy might make them go away for a while. But is it not rather like the burning of the bodies of witches and heretics for their own good? Their bodies might be ruined, but at least their souls might still be saved. *The Truth in Love* comes dangerously close to that way of thinking and that kind of world.

For those who find their sexual desires returning some months after conversion, they have, within the particular kind of 'Christianity' they have adopted, to say, "I've been tempted and I've fallen." What follows is often a despair that turns to violence against oneself – or an anger that turns to violence against others.

In her book *Lament for a Lost Enemy* (SPCK, 1978) Una Kroll describes how a student friend of hers was influenced by her 'enemy', at the time a convinced evangelical Christian. This student 'confessed' in a group of Christians that he had homosexual desires and was in love with another man. He was converted, but some time later his desires returned. He was so depressed that he committed suicide, leaving behind him a note to say that he couldn't face his continuing homosexuality being known by others, and that he preferred to take his own life rather than find himself, as he put it, corrupting other young men. Those who put all the emphasis on spiritual conversion rather than complementing it with a deepening understanding of one's sexuality have the suicides and attempted suicides of not a few human beings on their conscience.

On the other hand, the converted Christian may react in this way: "I've been converted, so it can't really be me that's doing these things again. I don't know *what* came over me. I don't know *what* got into me." We're back with the idea and the framework of impersonal invading forces, and the Devil conveniently at hand to be blamed. Sexual acts are again isolated from the person, put 'over there', with someone else responsible. By an ingenious sleight of hand the gay person who is content with life is seen as the Devil's agent, to be abused with excessive zeal and virulence. (The dogmatically zealous who wield dictatorial power in government are cast in the same psychological mould.)

Take this one stage further, and ask, What kind of God is implied by this framework of thinking and this kind of behaviour? Are we not here dealing with a God who will use force if necessary, the final sanction of destruction, and who delegates that power to those who are certain in their own minds that it is right to banish all gay people to a desert island? Would that such 'Christians' followed the One who showed us that God in the end will allow others to kill him and so attempt to extinguish love, rather than himself be the destroyer. He is the One who cannot use that ultimate weapon if his name truly is that of Love: there can be only one ultimate. That is not to say that Love cannot be stern, that there is no refining fire, needed by gay people just as much as by anyone else, to purge us of our persistent selfcentredness and pride. But it is to say that we must be very careful to have all the facts we can muster before we make even a hesitant judgment of another human being. We too often make the mistake of supposing that we can hate the sin and love the sinner. That's an easy distinction that actually dodges responsibility for disliking the *person* opposite you. And if you're on the receiving end, you know in your heart of hearts that the kindness is patronizing and unreal, and covers a great deal of anger against you. In one of Auden's poems, Joseph of Nazareth knows that people are talking about him behind his back, criticizing him and muttering: Mary's having a baby you know, and they're not married. He goes into a pub and orders a drink. Then he comments, "When I asked for the time, everyone was very kind." The hypocrisy of it!

You see, if I were to commit a murder, *I* would expect to be disliked, for who I am *includes* what I do. I may dare to hope that I may still also be loved for who I am by those who can bear the ambiguities of love and hatred within themselves. But preserve me from the bland smile which doesn't reach the eyes! And our sexuality is certainly complex and subtle and often double-edged. But Mr Johnston oversimplifies. He externalizes one particular act and then tries to see it as a thing separate from the person. It leads to a strange theology and demonology, as well as to a kind but patronizing surface attitude towards others that covers a violent hatred beneath. It is much better to be open about being enemies, that we hurt and hate as well as love and like. For I believe that the approach of Mr Johnston and Jef springs from a psychology of scapegoating and fear – fear of inner chaos and of unacknowledged anger and hurt, and from a theology of a God whose wrath is in the end greater than his love.

Where do we go from here? How do we cope without

destroying one another? For Mr Johnston thinks that all those in the Gay Christian Movement – and presumably also in *Gay News* – are, according to the Festival of Light booklet, employing "propaganda for promiscuity and sodomy", are spreading "moral poison" and "plague", are "degenerate" people who "smear" and "defile" friendship. The logic of the position is to use weapons of excommunication and exile. (Perhaps a hopeful geographical sign these days is that there are fewer places that can be 'countries of exile', beyond the pale, in the outback, though high walls can still effectively screen and banish the 'outlaws'.) Whilst not accusing Mr Johnston of wishing to pin pink triangles on the shoulders of all gay people, it is only too true that the less scrupulous can push the logic of his ideas to such extremes. Ideas and values, with their unspoken but real implications, form a structure of thought that enables others to be violent and destructive. Surface togetherness and kindness without truth and justice are but masks of tyranny. Apartheid is no less an insult to human dignity, nor any less grave an injustice, because it can be masked by personal kindness from white employer to black servant.

Can I love this enemy? Not that I can yet like him, but can I try not to destroy him? With a costly love of the will I am to keep in touch and strive with my enemy in the belief that he has somewhere a *blessing* to give. I can perceive one already: the opportunity to scour the depths of my own motives and of my understanding of God, to become clearer and so more helpful to others. And what blessing might I have to give in return? Well, once the enemy has had the patience to sit where I sit and listen, he may be glad that he has met people who are sensitive, caring, perceptive about life, open to the mysteries of God. Would that the Pilot could see – and receive.

6
The other country

To separate himself from the society of which he was born a member will lead the revolutionary, not to life but to death, unless, in his very revolt, he is driven by a love for what, seemingly, must be rejected, and, therefore, at the profoundest level, remains faithful to that society.

DAG HAMMARSKJÖLD: *Markings*

Michael Harding – closed and open secret

Michael Harding kept his gayness a closed secret for most of his short life. It was a great loss that he died just as that secret was becoming open, to his friends, his family, and the people of the parish and town where he served as a priest. It is now eight years since he died. He had begun to live his life in a way that brought his sexuality into the rest of his being and behaving. Whether you knew he was gay or not, he was a person full of life, someone you couldn't help noticing and whom you soon came to respect. When the very secular Housing Committee of Watford Borough Council wanted a name for a new side road opposite the church where he served, they remembered him and called the road *Harding Close*. I'm glad to have this opportunity of paying tribute to Michael and to try this afternoon to echo a theme that was part of his struggle and ours.

"Your decision as to whom and how much to tell probably depends on how friendly you are with a particular person, but complete secrecy can be a tremendous burden." That quotation comes from a pamphlet published by Abbott Laboratories which is called *Living with your Ileostomy*. In other words, how do you cope if you have to wear one of those plastic bags to take waste products from your body? You see that I'm being slightly coy. I didn't want to look at the pamphlet. I felt embarrassed and repelled. I can believe that you could easily feel it a stigma if you had to wear one. People might withdraw and keep their distance if they knew the truth. The booklet tries to reassure the 'sufferer': there are many of you around (even athletes); you can lead an ordinary life; there is nothing to be ashamed of.

I've heard that before somewhere. Whatever is kept secret in an atmosphere of fear and worry is a great burden, especially if you can see no reason why other people should want to withdraw. One of the quiet achievements of the Gay Christian Movement has been to live our own secret together more openly. For some of us this means that we no longer mind who knows.

Alan Turing and Radclyffe Hall – closed secrets

But let me go back and recall the atmosphere of some forty to fifty years ago. In the mid-1930's Alan Turing was showing himself to be one of the most brilliant mathematicians of his generation. He was such a superb 'thinking machine' that he became one of the founding fathers of the computer. But he was also a 'misfit': his intellectual life and his bodily life didn't match. He was homosexual in orientation, but his occasional attempts to make relationships were tentative and unsatisfying. He lacked any bodily awareness and language with which to approach others. He found elegance and truth in mathematics, but with the rest of his life he lived an awkward lie.

He belonged to an élite which gave this message to its favoured sons (and I mean 'sons'): "We will protect your sexual secret by closing ranks whenever possible, but we can no longer do so if you are 'found out' by anyone outside the closed circle." Such elegantly furnished closets are still to be found in universities – and in vicarages.

Andrew Hodges has written a biography of Alan Turing called *The Enigma of Intelligence* (Unwin Paperbacks, 1985). In it he writes of what it meant to live with such a secret, a stigma in the wider social atmosphere of the thirties. And remember that social stigma is far more powerful than the threat of legal penalty in damping down any open expression of opinion or way of life. John Stuart Mill pointed that out, and it is still relevant. What the neighbours think is more powerful than what the law says.

Hodges comments: "The general rule remained that of unmentionability above all else, leaving even the well-educated homosexual person with nothing more encouraging than the faint signals from the ancient world, the debris of the Wilde trials, and the rare exception to the rules supplied by the writings of Havelock Ellis and Edward Carpenter." (p. 77)

The stigma had similarly been at work over the publication in 1928 of Radclyffe Hall's novel, *The Well of Loneliness*. The title was chosen by her lifelong partner, Una Lady Troubridge, *not* because lesbianism of itself was bound to mean a ghastly lonely life, but because the isolation of the lesbian by society around led to an ever-present struggle with loneliness.

"The deprivation," Hodges goes on, "was. . . of the spirit – a denial of identity. Heterosexual love, desire and marriage were hardly free from problems and anguish, but had all the songs and novels ever written to express them. The homosexual equivalents were relegated – if mentioned at all – to the comic, the criminal, the pathological, or the disgusting. To protect the self from these descriptions was hard enough, when they were embedded in the very words, the only words, that language offered. To keep the self a complete and consistent whole, rather than split into a façade of conformity, and a secret inner truth, was a miracle. To be able to *develop* the self, to increase its inner connections and to communicate with others – that was next to impossible." (p. 78) Alan Turing carried within him a secret that was not even supposed to exist.

Meanwhile, with great irony, he became part of another secret world. There are a few people of whom you can say, The Allies would have lost the Second World War if it hadn't been for them. Alan Turing was one of them. Almost single-handedly he cracked the German secret codes used to communicate from the High Command to the patrolling U-boats in the Atlantic. He was at the heart of a world of secrets. In fact, "Churchill. . . . relied totally upon an unmentionable department, in which no one knew what anyone else was doing, and which made deceit into second nature." (p. 240)

That new bizarre world of secrets within secrets now has all of us in its grip, bound as we are by the nuclear phenomenon. No one individual *can* know it all, can even conceive of knowing it all. Sometimes I think that all our lives are controlled by the secret pulses of huge computers, working silently and invisibly. Certainly in our time we have seen the measures which are needed to keep secret and protected the missiles of genocidal power and the electronics of classified information. This is why intelligence work has continued on a war footing since 1945, and why the vetting of officials has become more stringent. This is why we continue in that ludicrous twilight in which homosexual activity among men is still so stigmatised that evidence of it – even rumour – can lead to blackmail and be thought likely to involve the exchange of secrets. The myth – or 'mythette', to use Hodge's word – of the homosexual traitor-spy still exercises fascination and power.

Alan Turing and Guy Burgess – secrecy and betrayal

Now Alan Turing was no traitor to his country. But others became increasingly worried that he might decide to become one. With benefit of hindsight, we might rather say that his country, the prejudice of the social climate in which he lived, betrayed him. Certainly there was betrayal in the way he thought of himself as a superb machine, but cut off from his bodily and sexual self. He continued to be at the centre of the nation's secrets for a few years after the war until the acquaintance of an acquaintance burgled his home in Wilmslow, near Manchester, in 1952. Naively he told the police, and in the investigation illegal homosexual activity came to light. He was put on probation and given hormone treatment. More seriously for him, he was now excluded from the only world that gave his 'mind' meaning, and there was not yet an historical or social context, such as we have begun to enjoy, in which the life of his 'body' could find meaning. In his isolation he took his own life on 7 June 1954, just two weeks before his 42nd birthday. At the time, no one could understand why. The picture I have given you from Andrew Hodge's biography simply could not have been drawn until a generation later, until the history of his time had become more fully understood, its secrets slowly coming to light.

Others of Turing's generation did of course become spies, and a few of them were homosexual. This is the theme of Julian Mitchell's play, *Another Country*. The Guy Bennett of the play is based on the historical Guy Burgess, of Burgess and Maclean fame. He recognized how the public school system played a game of deceit: homosexual activity could go on as long as no one had to know, but an open relationship of love with another boy – especially with a boy from another house in the school – could not be tolerated. Bennett's response was to adopt the game of deceit, and turn it round. In adult life he pretended to be loyal to his country, but in fact slipped secrets to a foreign power. He had been betrayed: he had been beaten at school, and socially ostracised, because a deep love was unacceptable. And he determined on revenge. In a way he was more aware than was Alan Turing, but he was just as bound by the climate of the day. The rules were the same. The shock waves that ran through the body politic when the truth came to light – from Burgess to Blunt – fed the myth of an inevitable connection between homosexuality and betrayal. The homosexual person is believed to be the hidden enemy within, spreading corruption and dissent. In so far as gay people today keep their identity a closed secret, they feed that myth.

(By contrast of course there is that other bit of mythical nonsense: *British* secret agents are fine, upstanding, dashing, loyal, gallant men and intelligent and beautiful women. St.

George rescues the maiden and slays the dragon and is called James Bond.)

However, as Andrew Hodges points out, there is a grain of truth in the "highly traditional equation between sodomy, heresy, and treachery." For the very idea of homosexuality is believed to undermine the social and political institutions of the day, not least that of "the family". In the 1950s, "in the post-war re-establishment of male employment and female domesticity, that threat became more conscious. To those who perceived marriage and child-bearing as duties rather than as choices, homosexuals appeared as the secret, seductive protagonists of a heresy, portrayed in religious terms of 'converts' and 'proselytising' and assumed, together with Soviet-inspired communists, to be plotting a conversion of the world. . . Meanwhile, the axioms of politics held that, granted the existence of an enemy, real or imaginary, any dissension or falling out of line could be regarded as weakening the state, and hence a form of treachery. And it was commonly suggested that a man who could do *that* thing, the worst thing in the world, was capable of anything. He had lost all mental control. He might love the enemy." (p. 500–1)

The myth remains powerful, far too alive and well for our comfort, especially in a decade of high unemployment, a renewed emphasis on the supreme value of the family, a careful cultivation of the foreigner as the evil enemy, and a pressure on women to keep to traditional roles, the 'Kinder, Küche, Kirche' of Germany in the 1930s: children, cooking, church. Radclyffe Hall's words of 1928 are true, but the struggle they refer to is far from over. She wrote of "a battalion" formed in the "terrible years" of the First World War, "that would never again be completely abandoned. War and death had given them a right to life, and life tasted sweet, very sweet, to their palates. Later on would come bitterness, disillusion, but never again would such women submit to being driven back to their holes and corners. They had found themselves." (*The Well of Loneliness*: p. 311: New York: Covici-Friede: 1928)

Trapped by the myth

So we need to be on our guard, and not allow ourselves to be sucked back and drowned by the undertow of the present ebb tide. After all, even on a conservative estimate there are two and a half million gay people in this country, and I have yet to see evidence that they are all spies. Unfortunately, the emotional power of myths has nothing to do with reason. Even if obviously false, they have a powerful effect. And we ourselves can be caught in the trap – precisely because of our own sense of having been badly let down, betrayed by 'them', whether through lack of accessible information about our history or numbers, or by the silence of schools, or by the heterosexual family in which we were almost inevitably nurtured. A long time back we must have sensed that we didn't somehow fit in. As we become more aware of our own individual past, we perhaps remember that we were on the fringe of forgotten conversations in youth club or pub. We knew that we weren't really acceptable, even when there was no actual hostility, just an ignorance and an ignoring – in which we ourselves at the time shared – of what anyway couldn't be obviously seen. And if you do not *know* your own truth, you *cannot* receive even such acceptance as *is* being offered. As you begin to realise what has happened, the seeds of a double life have already been sown, and for some the desire for revenge and betrayal. Many of us here will recognise the mood of these verses by two 19th century Englishmen: 'A.E.' and Oscar Wilde.

This is part of 'A.E.'s poem, *Germinal*:

> In ancient shadows of twilight,
> Where childhood had strayed,
> The world's great sorrows were born
> And its heroes were made.
> In the lost boyhood of Judas
> Christ was betrayed.

This is a stanza of Oscar Wilde's *Ballad of Reading Gaol*:

> Yet each man kills the thing he loves,
> By each let this be heard,
> Some do it with a bitter look,
> Some with a flattering word,
> The coward does it with a kiss,
> The brave man with a sword.

For each one of us who has responded to being betrayed by betraying our country, turning bitterness outwards, there must be hundreds who have turned the betrayal inside. They are the ones who have become consumed with self-hatred, who have found no one to talk to who was at ease enough to recognize them, let alone found anyone to love, and have taken their own lives. Many of us will have brushed, and sometimes still brush, the twilight world of deception and silence and isolation. It is the world of Graham Greene's *The Confidential Agent*, Mr D., "on the run, disreputable, sensing what it would be like to meet someone with whom he could be completely himself." Knowing no trust, he is the one who has lost hope of finding, "in the awful solitude of the desert, a companion."

The myth did its work well, reducing both women and men to images like that of the foreign spy, making us speechless in our own country. Thank God we have begun to speak in our language, having by some miracle found another. Now we can listen to our stories, and find courage to live our own patterns of life, at least to some extent freed from the myths of the past. We have had to learn that we do not speak the language of the heterosexual country in which we live. We do not have the same vocabulary and grammar. We can still find ourselves tongue-tied in church circles, not able to counter the blast of 'Sodom and Gomorrah' and 'St. Paul says in Romans'. But if a person can think of nothing but 'abomination', there is no effective argument which starts with that language: it is the very starting point and assumptions which have to be challenged. Those convinced that they are completely right find it impossible to listen to others of different views. In *that* situation, we can only, with passion, anger, and truth, tell our own story in our own way, and believe that there may just be a human being underneath our opponent who is more human than the views and opinions being expressed.

A new and virulent strain of the myth

We need to value steadily our own insights, stories, experiences, faith, and to nourish one another in these things, not least in 1985 because the myth is alive in a new and frightening way. I wish I needn't mention AIDS at all, but it is unfortunately with us and won't go away. And it will get worse. It fuels the myth with renewed prejudice, and is leading to rejection and horror. (I laughed at lunch-time when someone told me that he had been at a dinner party a few weeks ago, and when it came to light that he was gay, his hostess threw the crockery away.)

We are told that we have a hidden enemy in our midst, a secret subversive danger to the health of the nation, even to its very lifeblood. Remember how the Nazis wanted to purify the blood of the 'Aryan race' by eliminating everybody else? And worse: Andrew Britton has written, in the *New Statesman* for 15 March 1985, of how the disease has become attached to the great fear of our day, that of 'the end of the world': "Little effort is required in 1985 to cultivate the sense that we may all be dead tomorrow, and it has been so easy to define gay men – about whom everyone feels anxious anyway – as harbingers of universal death because universal death *is* actually what people are afraid of."

So readers of the popular press have been given a whole range of 'gut feelings' to direct towards gay people. Andrew Britton again, this time in *The Guardian* for 5 February this year: the suggestion is that "gay men are an insidious, all-pervasive, and *invisible* menace to the lives of ordinary human beings going innocently about their business."

Further, the use being made of the disease in society

connects all too easily with that other myth that homosexual activity is itself contagious, and, given half a chance, spreads like a prairie fire. All I can say to that is, Show me the smoke! Given the social climate, it's hardly an attractive proposition to be gay: we don't exactly have it easy, even without a new disease. The conversion rate of heterosexual people must be appallingly low and the lapses phenomenally high! And the favoured few in the charmed closed circles are hardly the ones to light prairie fires.

Of course secrecy about AIDS has hampered action against its spread. In fact gay people – and particularly the Terrence Higgins Trust – were the first to give information and advice in this country. Now the health authorities are catching up. But we have seen in recent weeks how hard it is for the public to be straightforward about it, what with corpses in sealed plastic bags and police refusing food prepared by a canteen cook who happened to be gay.

By contrast, I'm not aware of this kind of reaction to the equally rare and difficult-to-catch Legionnaire's Disease. I'd even thought it had something to do with the French Foreign Legion until I was told that the first cases were noticed among members of the American Legion who were participating in a conference in a hotel. They are the equivalent of the British Legion, and I don't recall any move to ban Remembrance Day Parades.

We need to think and act calmly, and not succumb to what Keith Waterhouse in the Daily Mirror referred to as AIPS, or AIDS Induced Panic Syndrome. Let's remember that the disease is rare and is very hard to catch, especially if simple precautions are taken.

(It's an odd thought, and I'm not at all sure what to make of it, but there are probably some people in this room who are at high risk from AIDS, as well as definitely some people in the lowest risk category of all: there are no known cases among lesbian women. The only women known to have been infected have caught the disease from men. That prompts the speculation as to exactly who is likely to be aboard the next Noah's Ark!)

Apart from being calm before the facts, what else can we say? Well, let us put the disease in a wide perspective. For all kinds of reasons, from commerce to evangelism, people have crossed frontiers and oceans. As the pace of exchange has increased this century, so has the spread of viruses once limited to relatively small areas. So the virus that can lead to AIDS possibly 'escaped' from its Central African home through sexual contact between an African and a Haitian. Well, remember that we took measles and syphilis to the Pacific and decimated island populations because their organisms were not immune. So missionaries often died of yellow fever in West Africa, having left Europe but a few months before. We live in a hazardous and risky time, and if we belong to a cosmopolitan company of people, we partake of this crisis of a clash of people and cultures more intensely than others. Of course it makes us more vulnerable to both culture shock and body shock: it also provides the opportunity for our lives to be enriched through friendships with people of varied hues and backgrounds.

Further, if AIDS makes us look death more clearly in the face, well, that is a Christian thing to do. The more we can be released from the fear of death, the more we shall be able to greet the present with joy and live it with love. But let us also be on our guard against a certain homosexual death-wish which makes some people blind to all precautions.

I wonder if this death-wish is connected with that deep sense of shame that seems inevitably bound up with sexuality in an imperfect world. Is there something distorted within us that whispers: You deserve what's coming to you. To this we have to say firmly that disease is *not* a punishment for sin. Yes, it is part and parcel of the gonewrongness of things, but it is not a question of a single effect of a particular cause. If that were so, everyone on this planet would have been wiped out a long time ago. Sexual sins have never been high on the Christian list of priorities, and acts of pride and malice should surely have led to many a devastating plague! No, to burden a person who has a fatal disease with unnecessary and intolerable guilt is unjust and cruel.

In the Gospel according to John, Jesus is recorded as explicitly saying that it was *not* because of a man's sins, nor those of his parents, that he had been born blind, but so that God's glory might be shown through him. Is there any way in which that can be said of the victim of AIDS? It sounds preposterous. Yet I wonder. At a time of deep crisis in a civilisation, an apocalyptic time, an 'end-time', it does seem that some people have to sacrifice more than they would choose to do – and on behalf of others. This is an interpretation that cannot be *forced* on anyone, but some might be able to choose to accept it. May it be that a few people, symbolically suffering that universal death that we all fear, can make us look that death more clearly in the face, feel the fear, allow it to melt inside us, and so let it become a power of love and will to make some sacrifices of our own for the sake of the earth's survival – sacrifices of time, energy, wealth – so that this world may come through the death-throes of an old order and the birth-pangs of a new one? The gateway to life has always been through a dying, both as individuals and as representatives of humanity. There are echoes here of the Suffering Servant of Isaiah Chapter 53 and of Christ on the Cross. These are deep waters indeed, but they may need to be stirred, however gently and cautiously.

The open secret of touch

More cheerfully, there is another response that we can make to the fact of AIDS, and that is to use the fear of this disease to make us more and not less affectionate with one another. I don't say this glibly. If friends of ours develop symptoms of AIDS, we are going to have the 'gut' reaction of 'Leper'. We will want to draw back. It will take courage to embrace a sufferer, and to keep on doing so. As an American vividly put it, the victim has to bear a social stigma the size of Manhattan. But the challenge in all this is for us to expose that old British secret commandment, Thou shalt not touch. On the contrary, Thou shalt! This is the first open secret for today. I very rarely take upon myself the temerity of the Old Testament prophet and say, Thus saith the Lord, but this is one occasion. The American author Merle Miller gave me the thought: Thou shalt not commit unloving: thou shalt touch.

On Thursday morning, I overheard a snippet of conversation at Aldgate East underground station. One black woman was saying to another: "She's got some good in her: you can feel it in your own body." This is authentic, and it is one of the secrets we need to learn and live more openly. Thou shalt be in touch. Thou shalt touch.

In this context, I wonder if we might meet Elizabeth Moberly on her own ground. She has the theory that we have same-sex relationships, not because of sex or sexual attraction, but because we are seeking to establish our own identity as masculine or feminine gender, which identity we are supposed never to have received from the parent of the same sex. Well, there may be some truth in that for some people. In most theories I've come across there is a grain of truth: the trouble is that they all seem to claim to be the last word. But let's suppose for a moment that this is an accurate 'diagnosis' of our 'condition'. The 'prescription' is a close, warm, physically affectionate relationship with someone, preferably heterosexual, of our own sex. Then, gender assured, we can go and make adult sexual relationships, with the 'other', ie. a person of the opposite sex whom we can see and relate to as a separate adult being in his or her own right. Now I don't happen to think that all gay relationships are a search for oneself in a narcissistic fashion, and in many such relationships I know of the partners seem perfectly well aware of the otherness of the other. But let that pass. We have a glorious opportunity to cure heterosexual folk of homophobia. You see, they now have a *duty* to come close to us, and we have the *pleasure* of coming close to them. Heaven knows where this may lead! Seriously though, those whose sexual activity has, for whatever reason – and there are many, not just AIDS – to be restricted, can find a different way of loving which is open to the extraordinary depths of intimacy that affection can bring. Can we offer *that* secret to those who believe that the only fulfilment equals freely available sex?

There are of course many ways of touch, many subtleties. And there is the touch that is trivial or mechanical or violent, where there is no personal meeting and where sex becomes a weapon. There can be a refusal to give of *oneself* through the touch. The one in effect says to the other: Refuse thou art, and to refuse thou shalt return. It is another expression of hatred. It is often the disastrous split of an Alan Turing taken to the extreme. When sexual activity is split off from the rest of the person and does not embrace the whole of the personality, any love of self or other is reduced to a minimum. The whole living organism is divided. We are out of tune whenever we behave as if we were just thinking machines or just a bundle of physical sensations or just pure spirit. Yes, we often *feel* like one or other of these 'things', but we are often unaware of what is happening to us. We become secretly subversive of ourselves without knowing it. We put our well-being at risk. We see this when a compulsion takes over, when a desire becomes so consuming that it threatens the whole of a person's life. So it seems to be with cancer cells that are 'suddenly' triggered into multiplying rapidly – maybe by stress, maybe by the organism as a whole saying, 'I've had enough.' Now I've no proof by western scientific standards, but I have a hunch that we are more prone to a breakdown of our immune system if we have 'attacked' our organism with too many antibiotics. I wonder if organisms do break down under the pressure of behaviour patterns that encourage this splitting apart of ourselves into compartments (and living in apartments?). In a sense we all suffer from this as human beings:

it is again part of the gonewrongness of things that we call original sin, the corporate sin that comes from our being bound together in communities and cultures. Indeed the very word 'diabolic' at root means 'split apart'. And we all have to emerge from those associations of sexuality with shame, guilt, hatred, punishment, and violence. Simply because our sexuality is so intimately related to the rest of our personalities, it is bound to partake of distortion. We cannot get out of that one with a flourish of brave words or self-righteous political action. Much of human life is just tragic.

By contrast there is the way of touch that is 'symbolic', a word whose root meaning is 'bring together', the way simply of love. It is the deep encounter which is the touching of two human bodies, organisms, persons: it may be the touch of a finger-tip or it may be a rhythmic riding of waves of sensation and feeling in orgasm. In either way, and in many others, there is a making of love, a mutual communion and trust, a giving of self, a willingness to let go of control, an acceptance of the whole of oneself, the giving and receiving of self in acts of union that are profoundly creative. It is a declaring of your self as an open secret trusted to the arms of another. It releases new life and energy.

So the *moral* question becomes this: What kinds of touch will encourage the maximum closeness of loving? For our sexuality, whether we express it in a particular relationship or not, is, beneath all the distortions, our God-given means of reaching out to others and making loving contact with them. This means that we have to blow the cover of a closed secret that is akin to the taboo on touch. For our society is not afraid of violent touch so much as of tender touch. Men in particular need to break this taboo: it is the way out of the cul-de-sac that assumes that one person has to be dominant and victorious over the other in a relationship. This is similar to the cul-de-sac of misogyny, that hatred of women that comes from men's refusal to accept the feminine in themselves.

'Disturbers' of the 'Peace'

To learn this kind of language, to refuse to let it remain in hidden code, is to make a small but subversive political statement, because it concerns something more corporate than just two individuals. For the cul-de-sac is even more dangerous: it is writ large in Auschwitz and Hiroshima, the ultimate empty victory of oppression and war, now extended to the lust for destruction of the good earth herself. We see in our own day more starkly than ever before the choice: the old myth of isolated secrecy and hostility, or the open secret of friendship. As gay people we have a vital and open part to play in the resolving of this issue. For in the end we have to say one of two things, either, "You are my friend, come what may," or "You may be my friend, but if necessary I will find a reason for killing you." I know the first option is idealistic, but it may become political necessity.

If you remove tenderness from human affairs, there is no place where excitement and sensation stop: they will lead to murder, and in our day to genocide. Sexually, this means a refusal to act out the language of tools and weapons, of dominance and violence. This is the message to the men. To the women it involves breaking the code of the closed secret that surrounds men's accounts of war. The women of Greenham challenge the men on the other side of the fence to turn from the deathly existence they represent to the exultant life they fear. The heroism and humour of war films – from *The Dam Busters* to *Dad's Army* – obscure the horror.

However, that is changing. That horror did come home to the American people, through television, at the time of the Vietnam War. Too many questions were raised for comfort. Peter Marin says of the veterans of that war: "They became suffering pariahs, not only because of what they have done but because of the questions it raises for them – questions which their countrymen do not want to confront, questions for which, as a society, we have no answers." (quoted in *And They Felt No*

Shame, by Joan O'Hanneson, Winston Press, 1983). The Vietnam Veterans Counselling Center has given this appalling statistic: more than 57,000 Americans were killed in Vietnam; many of those who returned home were not given a hero's welcome, and out of their disorientation and confusion a further 57,000 have committed suicide since the war ended. Are they further victims who have died as part of the death-throes of the old order and the birthpangs of the new?

To say these things *openly* in our society *is* subversive. No wonder members of CND are photographed at demonstrations and have their phones tapped. It's hardly surprising. And by just *being*, gay people raise similar disturbing questions. We let secrets out of the bag. Like the Vietnam veterans, we don't fit the society to which we both belong and don't belong. In the film *'Gallipoli'* two young Australians join up in the First World War, and the only time they dare embrace is in the trenches the night before they are to go over the top to almost certain death. Do men go to war because that is the only way they can create circumstances in which they can be intimate with each other? If so, that is too dangerous a secret. Of course, the more tender way is received by the fearful as 'flaunting'. Terry Minyard told the January gathering of GCM in Southampton that the Public Order Act of 1936 (passed as a means of containing the Fascists) had been used against two gay men who were kissing each other in Oxford Street in London. It was construed as behaviour likely to cause a breach of the peace. All you need is a policeman to say that two passers-by looked affronted. It reminds me of the woman in the Isle of Wight some years ago who claimed to have been so distracted by similar behaviour that she had absent-mindedly begun shoplifting. Yet such behaviour *does* disturb, not a genuine peace, far from it, but the so-called peace that goes under the name of the 'order' of the time being, the customary way of things in a society. It is not easy for any of us to examine the distortions of that order and take action to change them. But once you have seen the truth, you cannot sit back and do nothing without betraying your deepest self, let alone those who need your courage.

Women too are questioning another part of the so-called peace as they make us men aware of the secret sexual violence that they have suffered – the violence of the rapist, the pornographer, and the incestuous father. Such violence has been far more common than most of us realised, and it has remained hidden because of the power that men have traditionally had over women. The secret has been kept by men, and it is now being prised open by women. It is another example of distortion, not of sexuality as such, but of the violence and betrayal of trust that become bound up with sexuality. It does seem that violence is the only way in which men can keep at bay the affection of which they are desperately afraid.

We are called to participate in the most tremendous struggle, often a struggle for the simplest and most ordinary things. But if we are true to ourselves, this is where we find ourselves. Edward Carpenter, who at the turn of the century lived in this city of Sheffield, and just outside it, discovered here intimacy and affection undreamed of in his previous starched world of middle-class Brighton, Cambridge, and the Church of England. He wrote in 1923: "Only go far enough, deep enough, into your own nature, and you are sure to haul up something which will get you into trouble with the world." (*Angels' Wings*, p. 118–9) To blow the secret cover of an age-old defence against freedom, love, and tenderness, is to invite trouble. But then folk of faith, tough, stern, gentle, non-violent and forgiving resisters, have never been promised comfort.

'Spies of God'

In this struggle we are called, as gay Christians particularly, to
> . . . take upon's the mystery of things,
> As if we were God's spies. (*King Lear:* V.iii. 16–17)

God's spies – God's 'espiers': these are the spies who see more clearly than most. They are 'frontier scouts', ahead of the pioneering wagon train, exploring new territory, 'the other country'. Such spies are sustained only by the unspoken marks of recognition among them, a rare sense of belonging that does not depend on a piece of earth you can call your own. Only in one another can pioneers find 'home'.

Matt Simpson greets a fellow poet, Norman Nicholson, on the latter's 70th birthday. Nicholson has lived his whole life in the same house in the small town of Millom in Cumbria. For Simpson, Nicholson has looked a truth

> full in the face: that home's a *belonging* –
> continuity of slate and stone for you; for me
> a kind of luggage dragged around.

So we remind the majority of people that hearth and home, even kith and kin, are but temporary resting-places and never the first priority. We must not rely on them for security, lest we be called out tonight on a journey. Our true home is in God, not in a pie-in-the-sky heaven, but in a God who is revealed always as Future, beckoning people on from their idols of security, the Frontier Scout par excellence, calling some to live always on that frontier and so help to shape that future for the more timid to follow on afterwards and inhabit. God said to Moses, without making much sense, 'I Am Who I Am', or, 'I Shall Be Who I Shall Be'. Perhaps that means something like this: "I shall be there in the encounter which you cannot predict, but which you will recognise as the promised land."

I shall not easily forget two such spies, who 'espied far', though they may not have wanted to be called spies of God. I shall remember them because of two not very good plays, one on the life of Edward Carpenter, *Dear Love of Comrades*, the other a dramatic history of gay men, *As Time Goes By*. To see those plays was to recognise myself as a citizen of the 'other country', led on there by them, a land, or at least an oasis, flowing with milk and honey. They had been there before me, and beckoned me on. At such moments you know that there is no going back if you don't want to be turned into a pillar of salt. One of the playwrights was Noel Greig: the other, Drew Griffiths, was murdered on 17 June last year. He scouted out the promised land, but like us still journeying people, did not stay there long.

The painful secret of emptiness

It is no easy vocation to be a spy of God. We need to be consecrated spies, rooted in the end only in a God whose Love impels us into that unknown and insecure future. And we shall report back, not in whispers behind cloak and dagger, but aloud and openly. We shall even say that, though there is a club called 'Heaven' under the arches of Charing Cross, to go through those pearly gates is not to gain automatic admission into the Kingdom of God. We shall also report, from the heart of our fragile, and sometimes temporary, relationships, that part of the mystery of our human sexuality is that it never yields all of the union and creativity that it promises. There will always be a yearning that can never be completely satisfied. But there is no point in complaining about that. It is a fact of life. We have to let it settle in the heart of us, often as a secret wound, however open. Many will not be able to understand, but it may be that we shall have to be content with the occasional oasis of milk and honey, with the whisper of the thunder on a distant shore. For while a sexual relationship may give us more than we ever once dreamt possible, there is also a strange and wondrous gift in the secret mystery of sexual solitude, of its barrenness and emptiness. There is something that we receive only from the midst of an inner hollow place. I suspect that women know this more crucially than men, particularly those who have never borne children. Only when we know the place of emptiness can we experience the creative surge of the love and power of God within us – with no human fertilising. (Is this the truth of the Virgin Birth?) This will always be a secret nonsense to those who place continuity and control at the centre of their lives – *and* to those who think that continual sexual pleasure is somehow a right that should never be denied. Others may say, How can you possibly live without sex! How can you be happy without physical descendants! How dare you choose not to have children! But not to do so, and yet to live your sexuality, is to have the secret knowledge that you, the spy of God, are also the friend of God, for you follow God's own costly way.

These, then, are secrets, secrets to be made open, about touch, about emptiness, about a love that dares to speak its name. Can we as gay Christian people begin to sense a new confidence as we open these secrets, a new power, not to change the whole world, but at least to change a corner of it? It is a power that will be linked to passion and feeling and tenderness, a power that knows what it is to sacrifice, to be wounded, to give blood (if not for transfusions, at least for witness), the blood that is the seed of the next generation's flourishing, a power that comes from dogged endurance, a power that knows not to coerce and take advantage, not to control but to create and to love, a power that can sometimes hold back and embrace the folly of powerlessness.

The Other Country

This 'foolishness' is the divine folly of dreaming of and working towards a world in which we do, as so many fear, love our enemies. This, too, is a secret to be declared open. We are called to be spies who scout out the land, not to destroy the inhabitants, but to ask, What is their interest? What will help them most? What do we both need? How can I help rescue both of us from the spiral of violence and hate? Dare I recognise you, Mary Whitehouse, as my sister, and dare you recognise me as your brother? It will be a world of friends where there is no need for secrets, when we shall all, in the renewed image of God, know the secrets of all hearts and neither be ashamed of ourselves nor condemning of others or of ourselves. We shall struggle, and we shall make our own peculiar contribution, and yet in the end this other country will come to us, as with all the things of love and joy and creativity, as a gift.

This is not another version of the promise of heaven as a compensation for life being so awful now. I happen to believe that God is drawing us ultimately to a life beyond this mortal one, where our shimmering ecstasies will seem like slight shivers down the spine, and where the fearful power of the atom will seem but the impact of a blunt knife on diamond. But I am for the present content with a lesser vision of 'the other country'. Far too many Christians have used a belief in a future life to avoid doing anything about this one. And for now this world is where I see God at work, in history and not in eternity: it is this world in which God's agents, sometimes secretly, are at work for its transforming: matter matters, time matters, our story matters, and I see glimpses of the 'other country' here and now, not least in the very fact of this gathering today, undreamt of fifteen years ago. You see, I don't want to rely on security and safety in the future: faith takes risks. I don't want to relax into an easy sense of all being well one day beyond the bright blue sky. That cuts the moral nerve. It is moral, it is of God, to act well now, for its own sake, not for the sake of some future reward nor in fear of some future punishment. One day I trust I shall enter into my belief in life after death, but for now I lay it on one side, lest I cease to care.

God's Secret Agent

This shift also means that I need to jettison some of the baggage of belief I grew up with. One of God's secrets that is being revealed to us is that we have to leave behind images of God that tell of security and judgment, not to think of the Divine as Father, Judge, and King. You see, Love lets go, God's love lets go, that we might grow, that we might become ourselves the carriers of God, God embodied and earthed, sometimes hidden, incognito, sometimes openly disreputable to the powers that be, but living a liberating truth both in the depth of our being and in our public life. So did Jesus of

Nazareth. He lived a hidden life most of the time, and then lived the truth openly in the world, a world of enemies that meant that he had to suffer – and here is God's secret – but to suffer for Love's sake, to reveal Love as open and vulnerable, is not ignoble, and it leads to freedom and to life.

You see, I'm sure Jesus grew up sensing he was somehow different. I'm also sure he was an attractive figure, maybe not in a conventional way, but he drew others to him. He was going to be a leader, but the question he had to face was, What kind of leader? At some point he must have realised his secret of being a man completely at home in God. Was he then 'Messiah', God's special agent? Well, the title might do, but he was, it seems, reluctant to use it. It would mean adulation by the crowds, and suspicion from the powers that be. But he was not going to be the Warrior-King of popular expectation. No, he withdrew at crucial moments, and told people not to tell others about him. And when Peter says, "Yes, you are the Christ, the Messiah," Jesus immediately confuses all the disciples by saying that the Messiah is going to *suffer*. The secret is openly revealed, that God *is* suffering, vulnerable Love, but they can't see it: the shock is too great. It was like the shock that the inhabitants of a Pacific island had when Captain Cook's ship anchored in the bay. Because such a huge vessel was outside their experience, they just didn't see it. Only when the crew started to row ashore in shore in small boats did pandemonium break loose on shore. For the disciples, suffering and Messiah-ship did not, could not, belong together. Jesus realised that they couldn't cope, that no one at that time was going to understand, that he was from then on going to be increasingly isolated, bearing the open secret as a wound. So he was deserted and betrayed. Crucifixion simply made it all worse: if a man died like that, they believed it showed that he was cursed by God. Yet Jesus loved his own to the end, and his way was vindicated in resurrection. The pioneer of our salvation was made perfect through suffering. We do not yet see the fulfilment of that way of Love, but we do see Jesus, triumphant over all the powers of evil and death, releasing into the world that Love, the Love that was embodied on the Cross and embodied in a new dimension in the Resurrection. So we are offered our daily manna, we taste the milk and honey, and we are given courage to go on. It is the vision of God's secret in Jesus, the secret of suffering and vulnerable love, the secret of the love of enemies, the secret of a love that dares to speak its name, the painful secret of a love that is known only in emptiness, and the secret of simple touch.

Open Secrets

Let these things encourage us then, so that we do not disappear into the closets of fear. Let us not betray our companions nor our foes by a cowardly or over-prudent silence. Let us claim our place in the sun. There is still much more freedom to claim than we have yet done. Come out that little bit more – for your own integrity's sake as well as for God's. Of course we are at risk. We cannot escape the history and society of our time. Our freedom is not unlimited – nobody's is – but we are called to press the limits outwards, to give up our own close games of secrecy, of sexual cloak and dagger. We need to say to those who would turn from us, "Stay, listen, recognize me." If they won't, then we must, gently, insistently, boringly, be there with them, not invading them, but not invisible either. Keep claiming steadily, with Gay's the Word Bookshop, that it is *not* an offence to be open to the street, to the public world, with our identity, our history, and our claim that the world would be a better place if we were heeded. Of course we won't *approve* of everything that happens in the lives of gay people. We won't *approve* of everything in our own lives. We won't *approve* of everything a bookshop stocks. But to use that as an argument not to support our sisters and brothers is to fall into the trap of pretending to be perfect, a self-righteous moralism that is as nasty as anything in the 'Moral Majority'.

In the context of the Roman Catholic Church in America, James and Evelyn Whitehead have written about the way in

which gay Christians have come out there. "In so doing, their
life and vocation become a public witness of homosexual and
Christian maturing and a gift to the next generation. Such a life
provides for both homosexual and heterosexual Christians an
image of what it is to mature as a Catholic and gay . . . Where
there was once a void ('Do *you* know any gay Catholics?')
patterns of Christian homosexual maturing begin to appear.
It is possible! It becomes publicly imaginable to be both
homosexual and a mature Christian. Many believers have
known this for some time, but it was information not publicly
available, it was not part of the Church's social imagination.

"Closeted lives, however holy, cannot provide images and
models of religious maturing. A certain public exposure and
light is required for this virtue . . . to have its effect." (*Three
Passages of Maturity* in *Challenge to Love*, p. 184, quoted in
Concilium 173, 1984, p. 60–61).

A parable

When Alan Turing's world was closing in on him in 1952,
not a dozen miles away from Wilmslow, a ten year old boy
found himself in purgatory most Wednesday afternoons from
September to March. He had to obey the school rules and play
rugby. He loathed it, and even at that age once mistakenly
tried to change the rules by running the wrong way and
claiming to have scored a try at the wrong end. He longed for
snow and ice so that games would be cancelled. But most of the
time he couldn't escape the social reality in which he had to
live. He tried to bluff his way through, not to be too near the
game to be involved, nor too far away to be noticed. This was
not because he was secretly playing for the other team: it was
sheer fright. Six years later he and the other dregs occasionally
did manage to make up their own rules, like "There must be no
actual tackling." If your opponent managed to tap you on the
shoulder, you were to say, "Certainly, your turn," and hand
him the ball. It was infuriating to those who wanted a good
game. Of course we didn't get far, and we had neither the

desire nor the inventiveness to establish a new game with new rules. But the game of rugby started like that. One day in 1823 a boy called William Webb Ellis at Rugby School picked up a football and ran with it. He started a whole new ball game, as they say, and very soon they had to change the shape of the ball to an oval one that was easier to catch and hold.

The open secrets of the lives of Edward Carpenter and Walt Whitman

If you discover your unique sexual secret and yet try to hide it and live in the old ways, you will grow old with a harshness and hatred within that has led too many to a brittle and bitchy old age. Edward Carpenter saw its tragedy like this:

> Daily we pass, like shadows in a dreamland,
> And careless answer in the old curt tone,
> Till Death breaks suddenly between us, and
> With a great cry we know we have not known.
> (*Towards Democracy*, p. 300)

He himself lived differently, openly, knowingly, treating all whom he met as a friend. "If I am not level with the lowest, I am nothing; and if I did not know for a certainly that the craziest sot in the village is my equal, and were not proud to have him walk with me as his friend, I would not write another word – for this is my strength," (*Towards Democracy*, p.15)

That is not far from the friendship of God, and from the Jesus who enjoyed the company of the outcasts without asking them to change before he loved them. Carpenter longed for the day when gay people would "form the advance guard of that great movement which will . . . transform the common life by substituting the bond of personal affection and compassion for the monetary, legal and other external ties which now control and confine society." (*The Intermediate Sex*, p. 238)

That is idealistic, perhaps romantic, certainly a matter of faith. But is it impossible? Laughable? A nothing in the wind that whistles through the fence at Molesworth or down the corridors of the Customs and Excise? Edward Carpenter was himself inspired by another crazy-sane visionary, Walt Whitman. He is quoted as the epitaph to Alan Turing's story:

I know I am restless and make others so,
I know my words are full of danger, full of death.
For I confront peace, security, and all the settled laws,
    to unsettle them.
I am more resolute because all have denied me than I
    could ever have been had all accepted me,
I heed not and have never heeded either experience,
    cautions, majorities, nor ridicule,
And the threat of what is call'd hell is little or nothing
    to me,
And the lure of what is call'd heaven is little or nothing
    to me;
Dear camerado! I confess I have urged you onward
    with me, and still urge you, without the least idea
    what is our destination,
Or whether we shall be victorious, or utterly quelled and
    defeated.

All a speaker can do is to borrow some words and shape a few of his own. As Edward Carpenter said, it is like taking a neglected and dirty mirror, trying to wipe it clean, and placing it in your hands. Only you can tell me if what you see distorts or gives you some reflections of the truth.

APPENDIX 1: *Act of Worship*

This is an outline of the act of worship that followed the address:

1. A time of Remembrance
2. Hymn: For All the Saints
3. A time of Penitence
4. Hymn: Lord God your Love has called us here
    (by Brian Wren, from *Faith Looking Forward*, no. 6, Oxford University Press, 1983)

5. Readings from the New Testament
6. Hymn: Be still in God's Presence
7. A time of Silence
8. A time of Affirmations
9. Hymn: I vow to you, my friends of earth
10. The Peace, shared to the accompaniment of *Dona nobis pacem* by Mozart

The readings told of the stories of Judas and of Peter. The story of Judas' betrayal of Jesus and his subsequent suicide was drawn from John 13.21–30, Matthew 26.47–50, and Matthew 27.3–5. The story of Peter's denial and subsequent forgiveness and commission was drawn from Matthew 26.30–35, Matthew 26.69–75, and John 21.15–19.

The following are the words of Hymns 2, 6, and 9. Jim Cotter is indebted for inspiration and irritation to William Walsham How for the words of Hymn 2 and similarly to Cecil Spring-Rice for the words of Hymn 9: the authors may or may not accord with the sentiments expressed in the considerable re-working of the original text. The tunes used were *Sine Nomine* for Hymn 2, *The Ash Grove* for Hymn 6, and *Thaxted* for Hymn 9.

Hymn 2

For all the saints, who from their labours rest,
Who in the world their faith in God confessed,
Your name, O Jesus, be for ever blessed: Alleluia.

You were the Stranger in the dark of night,
With whom they strove to find their one True Light,
To whom you gave God's blessing ever bright: Alleluia.

They are the folk who gave with Love Divine,
Always in service did their wills incline,
Forgetting self, they did with glory shine: Alleluia.

They followed you, cast out the city's gate,
Killed by the eyes and guns of human hate,
Yet trumpets sound their resurrection fete: Alleluia.

And there will dawn a yet more marvellous day,
The saints with laughter sing and dance and play,
The Clown of Glory tumbles in the Way: Alleluia.

With earth restored, with this our fragile star,
In gladness home from pilgrimage afar,
We find in God a joy that none can mar: Alleluia.

(First written for All Saints' Church, Leavesden,
where Michael Harding served as a curate)

Hymn 6

Be still in God's Presence, be still in God's Presence,
Be still in God's Presence, and love and be loved. (*Repeat*)
Fall deep in the silence, fall deep in the silence,
Fall deep in the silence, the silence of God. (*Repeat*)

Hymn 9

I vow to you, my friends of earth, all worldly things above,
Entire and whole – yet broken – the service of my love:
The love that dares to question, the love that speaks its name,
That flowers still in barren ground, yet hides no more for
     shame:
The love that struggles through the pain, and whispers in the
     night,
Yet shares its secret with the world, to bring the truth to light.

This *is* that 'other country' we heard of long ago,
When called to be the spies of God where milk and honey flow:
A world where hurts find healing, where all th' oppressed run
     free,
Where friends who have been sore betrayed each other truly
     see:
It is our earth, transfigured, new, where wars and hatred
     cease,
Where spy and friend walk hand in hand in Christ our Lover's
     Peace.

APPENDIX 2

The Spy Stories of John le Carré:
An Appeal to Leaders in Church and State

Gay people ask of those in positions of responsibility in the Church and in other organisations a certain moral courage. Douglas Wallace (Director of the Center for Ethics, Responsibilities, and Values at the College of St. Catherine in St. Paul, Minnesota) uses the spy stories of John le Carré to make such an appeal in the context of large business corporations. His article, *John le Carré – The Dark Side of Organisations*, was published in the Harvard Business Review for January/February 1985. He writes of how le Carré acknowledges in his stories that there are two very dark facts about human beings. The first is that there is a gulf between individual human beings that inevitably makes us strangers to one another: there is a loneliness at the heart of each of us. Nothing can ever erase the secret mystery that we are to each other.

Coupled with this fact is another, and that is the way in which admirable ideals, intentions, and actions often lead to tragic consequences. Inevitably we betray ourselves and others. In the sensitive person this leads to sadness, and sometimes to penitence. As the enemy in the story is trapped, "he or she becomes all too human to the hero, and ourselves, stirring up deep feelings of regret and compassion." (Wallace, p. 7).

Our individual limitations, then, collide with fundamental flaws in organisations, and the collision spells tragedy. There is no way we can avoid it. We are often caught up in impersonal forces which more or less dictate our actions as individuals, and all the pastoral care in the world cannot hide this fact. It would be salutary if those in authority who, because of the nature of the organisations they represent, could acknowledge the tragedy in, for example, the refusal to give gay people certain jobs, or in having to move them elsewhere. It would be splendid if they could do more, but very rarely do we hear even this minimum acknowledgment. There are some who do not even seem to understand that impersonal forces operate at all, the smile in the left hand being unaware of the knife in the right.

If there is no way in we can avoid tragedy, is there any way in which it can be redeemed? Wallace refers to three scenes in the novels which include acts that suggest that once in a while there may be a hint of redemption.

"The first, found toward the end of *The Honourable Schoolboy*, describes the moment when Jerry Westerby must decide whether to follow through in his mission and help the secret service capture two enemies, who are brothers. Ko and Nelson are about to be reunited, perhaps permanently. Ko has found a way to escape his shady past, and join his brother whom he has cared for since birth. Westerby has uncovered Ko's past, and is about to entrap the brothers. But, when faced with the actual, human situation, when he sees the intensity, selflessness, and loyalty in their relationship, he decides to abort his mission. In the story he fails, but he did act, in favour of a loyal and loving relationship."

Friendship is our first loyalty, however often we betray our friends. (Anybody innocent in GCM?) We do betray, for reasons of pastoral discretion or political judgment, as well as from fear, and often the reasons are good ones; but we still betray. Occasionally, the primary value may break through. "You are my friend, and I will not kick you out or kill you." This is not a plea for favouritism, but a plea that leaders recognise the dilemma, and once in a while show that they are prepared to act according to their deeper convictions, at whatever cost to themselves.

The second scene is from *A Small Town in Germany*. "Alan Turner, the protagonist," writes Wallace, "has been trying to learn the truth about Leo Harting, who had disappeared, and what he had uncovered at the British Embassy in Bonn. Sick and feverish, he drifts back and forth between fantasy and reality, and finally, doubt."

In le Carré's words: ". . . The very facts which only hours before had brought him to the brink of revelation now threw him back into the forests of his own doubt. Yet how else, he told himself. . . is wisdom forged, and a course of Christian action resolved upon, if not through doubt? Surely, my dear Mr Turner, doubt is our Lord's greatest gift to those in need of faith?"

Wallace comments on this scene as showing the value of doubt to those in positions of leadership. Doubt makes us realise that our behaviour is always mixed in motive, and its consequences often beyond our anticipation and control; "doubt keeps our heads out of the sand." It also "implies a high degree of disciplined reflection, a consideration before the fact of the results of our actions on others." Lastly, it can reduce "our insensitivity and arrogance" and help us "become humble and more human". Gay people have suffered too much from what comes across – even if unintended – as self-righteousness on the part of those who exercise power.

The third scene takes us deeper still. It is from *Smiley's People*, where Smiley and his colleague Peter Guillam are waiting for Karla, the Russian master spy, to defect to West Berlin.

" 'If he comes, he'll come on time,' Smiley had said. Then why do we get here two hours early? Guillam had wanted to ask. Why do we sit here, like two strangers, drinking sweet coffee out of little cups, soaked in the steam of this wretched Turkish kitchen, talking platitudes? But he knew the answer already. . . . Because we owe the caring and the waiting, we owe this vigil over one man's effort to escape the system he had helped create. For as long as he is trying to reach us, we are his friends. Nobody else is on his side. He'll come, Guillam thought. He won't. He may. If this isn't prayer, he thought, what is?"

Wallace comments: "In this episode, le Carré invites us to recognise and respect as most important the human worth of those who are victims of betrayal in the modern world, even if we have taken part in that betrayal for all the right, organisational reasons.

"Le Carré uses two carefully chosen words in this passage, 'vigil' and 'prayer', that may perplex some of his readers . . . (He) defines keeping a vigil as a quiet act of intense focusing on the suffering or welfare of another person regardless of who he or she is or what he has done. It does not need to involve vocal communication; it requires presence. It is an act of emptying of self and identification with the center and spirit of another person, and doing so despite the fact that in many ways we are, inevitably, strangers to one another.

"To be strangers and yet intensely care for and identify with another person seems paradoxical and beyond our human capabilities; this is why Guillam talks about prayer. Keeping vigil is a transcendent act that is enabled by something beyond our limited human capacities. Prayer, in this sense, is recognition of something beyond ourselves that makes it possible to keep vigil for a stranger."

Again, do leaders in fact show evidence of standing by those who have been hurt by the organisation, especially if they have in part been responsible for the rejection? Do they keep vigil, do they pray? Do they in some small symbolic measure show that they care?

Is friendship the priority in values, is humble doubt a mode of professional life, is there any sign of care for the victims of betrayal? If so, gay people would then at least feel recognised in a fallen world, even if not exactly affirmed in their potential contribution to the life of the corporate organisations in our society.

7
What can bishops say about gay priests?

Last Christmas I received one of those cards which are sold in aid of a number of charities. One of them was the Rare Breeds Trust. Some bishops try to reassure their dioceses that gay priests are a rare breed and wish they were extinct, Well, I refuse to be like the dodo, and I suspect that priesthood and gayness are more resilient even than bishops. A former ordinand I know tells me that he has tried so hard to be an atheist, but cannot get away from the challenges posed to him by Jesus Christ. But he is no longer a member of a local church. An American cartoon shows two men with arms round each other talking to a bishop at a cocktail party, and one of them says, "Well, it was a choice between homosexuality and priesthood, and I took the more spiritual option." Is that choice necessary?

What can bishops say about gay and lesbian priests? I have mused on what the Lambeth Conference of 1998 might say, the bishops including for the first time three women, and one openly gay man. We, the bishops of the Anglican Communion throughout the world, having listened to one another, and having listened to gay people, priests among them, and having shown by our words and deeds that we have shared their pain and so claim some authority to speak, now wish to offer the following statement, in penitence and humility.

(Ah well, why not dream? You will have to distinguish in what follows from what could be said now, what might be said sometime in the future, and what are quizzical asides which owe more to the whims of the speaker than to anything bishops might conceivably say.)

We recognize that we have had to struggle to counter much of our inheritance that has given the impression that on the whole sexual activity is unfortunate if not bad. We have been

infected by the distortions of the past that have led us to believe
the only purpose of sexual intercourse to be procreation. We
have been too suspicious of pleasure. We have only recently
come to understand that sexual intercourse can help to sustain
a relationship, each partner nurturing and healing and giving
delight to the other. We have been repelled and offended by the
sight and sensations of sweat and semen. We have unthink-
ingly regarded sex as an activity that pollutes, from which we
need to be cleansed. Many of us earlier in our ministries used a
form of prayer for women after childbirth, that they might be
purified. From this perspective it is no surprise that we
regarded same-sex relationships as completely unacceptable.

Those of us who are English have had an extra difficulty in
clearing our minds about these things. Many of us were
educated in single-sex boarding schools and spent time in the
Armed Forces, and from what we were aware of in dormitories
and barracks, we have a mixed emotional memory of pleasure,
disgust, fascination, and guilt. [Ten years ago, some of us were
urging the government of the day to abolish public schools if
they wished to discourage the promotion of homosexuality.]
Of course from this perspective we were hardly aware that
lesbian relationships exist and had never met such couples. It
seemed as if everything we said was imbued with a kind of
fundamentalism about the goodness of one particular
heterosexual genital position. We repent that one of our
number (Salisbury, in *Christian* in October 1987) claimed that
our "sexual orientation needs to conform to this physical
datum," and that another (Norwich, in the *Sunday Times*, 3
January 1988) revealed how much his judgment was based on
his feelings when he wrote: "The popular image of the
frustrated spinster and the bachelor whom one suspects of at
least latent homosexuality is a distortion and debasement of
perfectly normal human beings." Many of us shared those
viewpoints and we now realize how oppressive we have been of
so many of our fellow human beings.

We have slowly come to realize how disembodied the

Church has been. Looking at the group photographs taken of the Lambeth Conference over the decades, we have to admit that we have looked like talking heads hiding the rest of our anatomies underneath a weight of sexually ambivalent robes, and cut off by our dog collars from all that happens below the neck. There are few powerfully and gently erotic human beings amongst us. At least the increasing proportion of coloured bishops has brought some affectionate warmth to our gatherings, and the women amongst us will not allow us to be too cerebral and heavenly-minded.

Of course we haven't until recent years been forced to admit publicly that any of the priests in our dioceses are homosexual in orientation. We have known that they exist but we have encouraged them to be celibate or discreet, depending on our conservative or liberal approach. And we have always insisted that their sexuality remain totally private. If they have been vicars of evangelical persuasion they have pretended to be heterosexual bachelors and have led their parishes in the mould of the hierarchical and military male authority figure. If they have been of more catholic persuasion, they have built cliques amongst themselves, and have often been despising of women. In some parishes a number of people have known of their sexual orientation, but these have usually been communities of those whom the dominant macho culture would define as 'weak', ie. failed men, women, and women-in-disguise wearing lace cottas with gold thread. We have also become aware of a few parishes where the priest has been openly gay and been striving for justice for the discriminated against in the parish, eg. coloured people or the umemployed. Here men have tolerated their sexuality because of the fight for justice and women have been glad of a relationship with a man which has no sexual implications. But our main impression has alas been one of hiddenness, frustration, lies, and fear, leading to a deadening of faith, a loss of enthusiasm for ministry, and an embittering of spirit.

We have to admit that we have been led astray by our own

limited perspective. We have tended to *see* only one thing – a particular sexual act between two men – and have failed to realize how complex and ordinary same-sex relationships are in most people's lives, priests and laypeople alike. We have been challenged by couples of the same sex who share a home and sexual intimacy, and as we have come to know them we have had to realize that the scriptural texts which we thought were conclusive have no connection with the lives of these our fellow Christians. Yes, we are all doubtless guilty from time to time of idolising, exploiting, and trivialising another human being, even perhaps of violent abuse, but we now see that homosexually orientated people are no more guilty of these things than heterosexually orientated people. Nor does their behaviour necessarily lead to that disintegration of the personality and of relationships that we believe to be the very opposite of God's will, the intention in ceaseless creative work of bringing harmony out of chaos.

What has really surprised the historians amongst us is the research that has shown that the Church in the past has been more tolerant of same-sex relationships than we have thought. Indeed, we now see that it is part of the tradition we have inherited that such relationships have been blessed in ceremonies in churches. We are particularly grateful to the Roman Catholic scholar, John Boswell, Professor of History at Yale University, for having alerted us to this evidence.

Of course *some* of us still find *some* kinds of sexual activity, either homosexual or heterosexual, emotionally offensive. But we do at least recognize that emotional reaction is not a good basis for considered opinion. We have used the word 'unnatural' too glibly, and it has usually meant either a custom socially unacceptable to us or behaviour that upsets us. Neither of these uses provides a basis for a valid argument. Further, we have come to understand that 'natural' must not be interpreted in a static way, as though 'nature' was built on some kind of mechanical clockwork principle rather than the dynamic everchanging process we observe and are part of. What we do have to examine, however, is whether particular customs and behaviour increase disorderliness and disintegration in the processes of "nature", or increase order and harmony.

We also have to admit that the argument about what is unnatural has been used (and backed up by scriptural texts) to condemn lending money at interest, to justify white people dominating black people, to justify men always having ultimate authority over women, and to condemn the eating of certain foods. (It is thought that the Anglican Church has never made much impact in France because English people have found the eating of snails to be a disgusting, stomach-churning, unnatural habit and so have offended French hospitality: the French have been heard to argue that to refuse hospitality is most unnatural.) We now recognize that we come to moral decisions over matters of finance, food, and political and sexual issues in more complex ways.

So we see that Scripture, Tradition, and Reason, those three pillars of Anglican decision-making, do not, as we once thought, unequivocally condemn same-sex relationships, and may indeed in some circumstances be held to support them.

It is precisely on these grounds that some of our brother bishops, at the time a dissenting minority, in the American Episcopal Church, issued a statement at their General Convention in 1979. We associate ourselves with this quotation:

"We are . . . deeply conscious of, and grateful for, the profoundly valuable ministries of ordained persons, known to us to be homosexual, formerly and presently engaged in the service of this Church. Not all of these persons have necessarily been celibate; and in the relationships of many of them, maintained in the face of social hostility and against great odds, we have seen a redeeming quality which in its way and according to its mode is no less a sign to the world of God's love than is the more usual sign of Christian Marriage. From such relationships we cannot believe God to be absent.

"Furthermore, even in cases where an ideally stable relationship has not, or has not yet, been achieved, we are conscious of ordained homosexual persons who are wrestling responsibly, and in the fear of God, with the Christian implications of their sexuality, and who seek to be responsible, caring, and non-exploitative people even in the occasionally more transient relationships which the hostility of our society towards homosexual persons – with its concomitants of furtiveness and clandestinity – makes inevitable."

At one time, in an effort to be pastorally sensitive, some of us quietly tolerated same-sex relationships within the Church, but we did so on the grounds that though any sexual expression was always wrong, it could be the lesser of two evils, not so bad as exploiting or trivialising another. Then some of us came to see that sometimes same-sex activity was wrong but that sometimes it could be held to be good, though the lesser of two goods. We used the analogy of remarriage after divorce. At least we realized that people of the same sex do fall in love and form relationships. Now we see that we do not need to make that kind of comparison at all. Just as we recognize that the fact of being married says nothing about the quality of that relationship, so we have found that 'in its own mode' a gay relationship can be every bit as good as many marriages. As in our understanding of 'nature', so with relationships: they are in process and they change over the years, and our concern should be with their 'becoming' as much as with their 'being'.

So gay people have shown us that we must no longer use phrases like 'the self-confessed homosexual', as though such a person were like a self-confessed thief. Rather should we use the word 'self-affirming', like a self-affirming woman, or a self-affirming black person. And we should think of sexual activity not by comparing it with theft (marginally justifiable perhaps, in extreme circumstances), but with acts of hospitality and sharing meals. We then have to take care that the boundaries of such hospitality are recognized and that it is not abused, so that such acts are truly ones of trust, intimacy, communion, healing, and celebration, and not occasions of betrayal. Our horror at the murder of Duncan while he imagines himself to be an honoured guest of Macbeth and our horror at the sexual abuse of children both stem from the pain and chaos caused in human life when a sacred trust is betrayed.

We wish to state again that the Church has over-reacted emotionally to openness about sexuality, and that we must not allow our feelings to dictate our judgements. After all, we have got used to the fact that priests do marry and presumably enjoy sexual intercourse – we do not wish our Church to adopt the unjustifiable position of Rome that all priests should be celibate, nor do we wish to limit the occasions of intercourse to those we hope will result in conception (though some of us were brought up to think of sex solely in that way). We ourselves have been comfortable with the experience of making love privately with our spouses on Saturday night and presiding publicly at the Eucharist on Sunday morning. We have not felt that we needed cleansing from an impure and polluted act before we joined with our fellow Christians in celebrating the love that God makes with us. So we claim there is no *reason* to be offended by the knowledge that a gay priest has slept with his or her partner the night before, or that a priest at the altar is pregnant.

We wish to be heard strongly on this point, especially as we have seen too much scapegoating of those who are different by those whose disturbed feelings rise to the surface and are expressed in hatred. Repression of homosexual feelings has been a characteristic of military and political males in European societies, a repression which led them to load their guilt and self-hatred on to those who were obviously or openly gay. In some the repression did not entirely work, and they have been the ones whose homosexual activity has been vicious and cruel, usually kept private until 'scandal' burst upon them, while in public they have been politically right wing and calling for punitive measures against sexual or racial groups. As a Church we express our pentitence and sorrow for the ways in which we have contributed to that discrimination and have so often led our priests to fear us as much as they have feared the prejudiced and unscrupulous in their congregations and local communities. We recognize that we have persecuted people not for their misdeeds, supposed or not, but simply because they belong to a category of people. So we have to our shame stigmatized black people, Jewish people, and women, as well as gay people.

We have wished that the whole issue would quietly disappear and we were surprised (perhaps we shouldn't have been) when we found ourselves so much in the forefront of publicity a few years ago. It was of course our own fault. We had not realised that we could not put the genie Freud back into a nineteenth century bottle, nor that so much of our refusal to talk about sexuality was based on fear and distaste. We have wrongly accused gay people of flaunting their sexuality when we really meant that we were disturbed because they were refusing to let us ignore the fact of that sexuality. We were foolish to be offended by the sight of two men kissing at a railway station or on a spring afternoon in the park.

In coming to terms with this scapegoating of which we have been guilty, we began to get used to the idea of sexual variety. At first we did this by recognizing that sexual activity often lessens in intensity and frequency as a relationship settles down. We came to accept a relationship from the point of view that it offered gay people the best opportunity of being healed of their emotional wounds of the past, much as a marriage does. We admittedly found it hard to be straightforward about the lustiness that is present in any sexual encounter, suspicious as we were of pleasure and passion. But one of our number, now in retirement but some years ago Bishop of Birmingham, Hugh Montefiore, wrote in *The Times*: "In such a relationship, the issue of genital acts would cease to be of prime importance, and as the relationship matures it may actually cease to be relevant at all." (20.2.88) This certainly helped some people get over their initial feelings of distaste. And one of us was amused to receive this letter from one of his priests: "I think you would like to be informed that I share my home with Chris, my beloved partner. But you will be relieved to know that we do not participate in the one act which seems still to cause you problems. Consequently, I think you will agree that there is no need for me to offer my resignation." At the time lesbian priests did not need to write at all. We did not know of their existence and in any case the particular act we had in mind naturally did not apply to them.

We must no longer ignore or minimise our sexual energies. We must not try to return them to the unconscious, repressing or suppressing them. What was unacceptable long ago was placed in an annual ritual on the scapegoat, on to Azazel, the goat-god, who symbolised sexual and aggressive energies. Rather do we have to recognize these energies openly and use them to love others accurately, powerfully, and intimately.

This was particularly important at a time when people with AIDS were being treated like lepers of old. We had to grow up quickly and become mature enough to face our disturbed feelings about sex, blood, bodily fluids, disease, and death, and not deny these troublesome parts of life by quarantining or distancing or punishing – either others or parts of ourselves. We had to face our fear, a fear which was all the more powerful in a time of economic and political insecurity, fear of invasion by the twin invisible enemies of viruses and radiation. This is where we began to learn from history. Medieval Europe, faced with economic collapse and the advance of Islam, sought to blame someone – and they persecuted women – the strange ones they called witches – and Jews, and heretics, and – well the words homosexual and gay weren't invented then – men who engaged in unusual sexual activity. An interesting historical footnote is the derivation given in the Shorter Oxford Dictionary of the word 'bugger' – it comes from the Latin bulgarius, meaning Bulgarian, heretic, usurer. We do not wish to scapegoat the few Seventh Day Adventist Eastern European bankers of our acquaintance.

To scapegoat is to treat someone or some category of persons as less than fully human. In the past we have thought that women have been less fully formed than men, Jews less human than Christians, homosexual people less human than heterosexual people. Against this we affirm the neglected Christian tradition of loving the ones our darkened minds would wish to label as our enemies, especially the enemy within, those feelings of fear and sexual guilt that we could not cope with and which we projected on to the vulnerable.

We have heeded the warning of Primo Levi as long ago as 1958, writing with the calm authority of one who had survived Auschwitz and who dared to look long and hard at what had happened and who sought to interpret its meaning.

"Many people – many nations – can find themselves holding, more or less wittingly, that 'every stranger is an enemy'. For the most part the conviction lies deep down like some latent infection; it betrays itself only in random, disconnected acts, and does not lie at the base of a system of reason. But when this does come about, when the unspoken dogma becomes the major premiss in a syllogism, then, at the end of the chain, there is the concentration camp. Here is the product of a conception of the world carried rigorously to its logical conclusion; so long as the conception subsists, the conclusion remains to threaten us. The story of the death camps should be understood by everyone as a sinister alarm-signal." (From the preface to *If this is a man*, Bodley Head, 1960.)

More specifically on our theme we were glad of the shock that Michael Snelgrove of *Catholics with a Right to Respect* gave in 1987: "The great threat to marriage, the family and society's moral health comes not from homosexuality, but from *male violence and sexual abuse, rooted firmly in a* DISORDERED MALE IDENTITY. *How long can the teaching Church, overwhelmingly male in outlook, neglect this serious objective disorder?*"

We now admit that our own conception of what we called homosexuality, what we saw, our actual perception, was limited and distorted, and we for long refused to see because we did not want to face up to the implications of change. And we did not see that our collusion with blinkered assumptions led us, often without meaning it, to speak with patronising slogans and selfrighteous rhetoric, and so make life more difficult for the confused, the uncertain, and the vulnerable. And we would wish to honour those who stood up and refused to be scapegoated, who refused their consent to our interpretations, and who gently and firmly and openly claimed their place in the sun. Many of them were hurt, and we have reaped the benefit of their sacrifice. No longer would any of us agree with the bishop who, in proposing an amendment to a motion in the Church of England's General Synod in 1987, expressed the conviction that homosexual relationships were always sordid.

We have taken the rebuke of Jack Dominian to heart. Early in 1988 he wrote in *The Tablet* (23 January): "Pastorally . . . both Rome and the General Synod of the Church of England have the wrong starting-point when they focus on genital sexual intercourse. What matters is people and their relationships. Homosexual men and women, created in the image of God, are as much in need of stable and loving relationships as their heterosexual counterparts, and the principal aim of society and Christianity should be to do everything possible to assist in this, rather than condemning. Within stable and exclusive relationships which make possible sustaining, healing, and growth, abstinence can be encouraged for those who accept the scriptural interpretation."

It has been a difficult journey, full of pitfalls. The power of sin, the refusal to allow our troubled darkness to come into the light, made us exclude people from membership and ministry, an exclusion that was backed up by unjust laws. Those who stood up and were counted had to face the reality that the excluders had more power – ourselves, God forgive us, among their number. We recall now that Jesus refused the power that dominates rather than liberates, and he identified himself with the excluded. It was not that he wanted to be a victim in a masochistic way, but that he realised the implications of his message of inclusion and was willing to bear the consequences. As one who identified with the excluded and who kept his heart open in love and truth to his oppressors, being willing to forgive them for their blindness, he drew the sting of their hatred and ultimately allowed them no power over him. He brought the dark game of dominance and submission, of self-righteousness and scapegoating, of our fears of sexuality and aggression, into the light, so that it would become so clear to us that we would no longer need to repeat it. It is taking us a long time to learn that lesson. So some of us still have to become identified with the excluded, to give up coercive power, and to seek like Gandhi to shame and isolate the powerful into impotence. Of course this has not always worked, and we have also had to strive for a change in the law, so that where hearts have not yet been warmed, and eyes not yet opened, the law can restrain the worst excesses of the powerful and protect the weak and the vulnerable and guard legitimate privacies. Good laws about sexual activity are like good laws about national parks – they protect a vulnerable landscape while at the same time enabling people's enjoyment. And even good laws cannot guarantee that individuals will act with wisdom and discernment, appreciating the need for boundaries to their behaviour.

We too as bishops still have to bring in the force of law from time to time. If a priest's behaviour is such as to render his or her ministry impossible or ineffective, if that behaviour is inordinate in that it affects his or her ability to lead and represent the local Christian community, then there has to be some means of withdrawing authority to minister. We have however learned much about how to say No. We always include a number of people in the process, especially the priest concerned. We realise that our power can distance us and feel oppressive. We wish to encourage that freedom that has been described as right relationships among us all, with everybody concerned participating in power and decision-making, and always with arbitration in the background. It is patronising to say that we will lose a night's sleep if a person's livelihood is at stake. So we try to work with that person with the aim of discerning a more fulfilling Yes in what will be a different future, into which the present No can be taken up and transformed. It seems to us that judgment is creative only if there is a vision before us of something more attractive and compelling, more demanding and satisfying, than the one we currently perceive. (In changing our minds about gay relationships, it was of course precisely that kind of vision that was a creative judgment upon *us*.). Also we acknowledged that any authority to say No over sexual issues would have weight only if we were seen to act over matters of clerical arrogance, pastoral incompetence, and collusion with inordinate greed.

[It is at this point that we wish to refer to another report from this conference, that on our discussions about the Virgin Birth of Jesus, another contentious issue which is bound up with our confusions about sexuality. It seems to us that this tradition has been intertwined, perhaps fatally, with a deep suspicion of sex. Remember that we used to think that the sexual act defiled a person, and that a woman needed purifying after childbirth, that a woman was not as fully human as a man, that the entire new human being was contained in the male seed, the woman being but incubator. If Jesus is God incarnate, then it would seem the only possibility, given these assumptions, that God as it were provided the lot, miraculously. For the first century, God could not have become incarnate in a woman for then he would not have been fully human. A sinless man's conception would necessarily have had to bypass an impure act. For us, it all seems to make Jesus less than fully human, ironic as that thought is in relation to our history of scapegoating. To be fully human is to be close, intimate, in bodily fluids always close both to new life and to death. We cannot yet present to the Church a common mind on these matters, but we do ask people to look clearly at the possibility that Jesus could have shown us what it is to be both fully human and fully divine by being born of a liaison between Mary and a handsome stranger whom she and Joseph (the latter by a dream) became convinced was a messenger from God, which is what 'angel' means. If so, the suspect circumstances of his birth would have even more clearly identified him with the poor and the outcast. And it may not be inconsistent with Christian faith to accept that he may also have been homosexual in orientation, since he was not as far as we know married (very unusual for a Jewish man), nor did his people have a tradition of celibacy. However these things may have been, we do realize that we have often presented to the world an anaemic Jesus, a pale sexless Galilean, and this has been another factor in making it hard for us to accept that we are all called to be sexually alive human beings in all our relationships, however much our particular vocations may call for a restrained sensitivity to others in the expression of that sexuality.]

For a long time, the approach we now take to gay relationships was not even talked about, let alone understood and accepted. Large bodies of people do not change their corporate mind easily or quickly. Indeed the pace of change has been rapid compared with the quite recent past, and although many think we did not change quickly enough, we are aware that there are others who think we have been hasty. But we realised that we could no longer remain as we were, hoping the challenge would go away. For a time we argued against it, and then began to open the door to a new approach. It made the job of a bishop a tough one. We had to be loyal to our inheritance, consolidating the best of the past, we had to learn resilience and humour in keeping the conflicts open and holding together those who were at odds with one another, and we had to allow the future room to breathe.

Some of us were accused of double standards, as in this

extract from a letter which we received which helped us to clarify what was going on.

"If you argue that double standards should operate in the Church, e.g. no remarriage after divorce for clergy, and you parallel this with same-sex relationships, i.e. no for clergy, possibly for laity, you are going beyond a liberal political tactic for softening the process of institutional change. For embedded in the comparison is the assumption that no same-sex relationship is better than having one, and you are implying that such a couple in the congregation are second-class citizens. Lesbian and gay people would not accept that claim. I frankly do not see the value of trying to compare marriage with a same-sex partnership. Even if the former is in some sense 'better', unless all same-sex, partnerships are 'sordid', as the Bishop of Chester claimed in his speech to the General Synod of the Church of England in 1987, i.e. that they are totally bad, there must be some good in them. If so, and they are compatible with Christian faith and practice, then they are as appropriate for clergy as for laity. That has yet to be recognized, even if those in the van of change, like women who sincerely believe that they have a vocation to ordained ministry, are asked to make sacrifices for the sake of the unity of the whole body of the Church. But choices have to be made eventually, and the pain of change and growth shared amongst us all. I still challenge those in ecclesiastical power to set the Christlike example of risking identification with the op-pressed, and to be known to enjoy their company. Otherwise, you have no authority to ask for sacrifices from lesbian and gay people, priests or laity, for they will discern you as over against them and never having listened."

That was no easy lesson in humility, and some of us found it easier to allow experiment than others. Not all of us were temperamentally like Gamaliel, who was secure enough in faith to allow something new to find its own level in the common life. But some of us found ourselves able to encourage the new vocal minority and were able to say to them, We need you to go against the grain of what now is: we are mature enough to ask you to begin to show us how we should change. Without you we should become fossils. We also learned to share power and leadership more. The whole issue of gay priests became much easier when people stopped putting them on pedestals or scapegoating them, and when leadership became more modest in its aims and practice and allowed the variety of gifts in Christian communities to flourish. We ourselves have become less 'lordly' we hope, and have tried to be more the servants of the servants of God. We have become less of a separate caste. It took the ordination of women to show us how foolish men look in dog collars and mitres. And the talents of certain gay priests have come into their own now that everybody is encouraged to wear gorgeous party dress at Christmas and Easter. Hierarchical and gothic ways have been collapsing ever since Jung dreamed that a turd from heaven had demolished Basel Cathedral, ever since we realised that for many people the great west doors of cathedrals were frowning and forbidding and excluding, ever since the collapse of heaven as a world separate from the rest of the universe, ever since the music of Christendom collapsed at the end of a song composed by Schubert, when what started as the melody of an evening hymn disintegrated as the wanderer on his winter journey realised that there was no hospitality for him even in the graveyard that in his hallucinations he had mistaken for an inn. We have presided over a period of upheaval every bit as revolutionary as the one heralded by Copernicus, and it is something of a miracle that we are still here to try and commend the ways of the God of Jesus Christ who does not know how not to love. Now we know that love has to include the contradictions and celebrations of our varied human sexuality. And in coming to these conclusions we wish to acknowledge too the help given us by scientists who have observed the patterns of the universe anew, by the space travellers who have shown us a small and blue and beautiful world to cherish, with an incredible richness of plant and animal and human life, by black people, women, and lesbians and gay men, who have shown us a more humane way to live.

In all these agonies and glories of change, the gay priest has had a particularly valuable part to play. It was pointed out to us that most American Indian tribes have given an honoured place to the persons in their communities who in some way, physically or psychologically, showed characteristics of both genders. They were neither hunters and warriors, nor mothers rearing children. They were 'threshold' people, and were to be found as teachers, helping people over the threshold from childhood to adult life, as healers, on the boundaries of illness and health, and as shamans, as priests, at home on the boundaries of death and life. They stood on the threshold, conducting people through their rites of passage. No fuss was made about their own sexual relationships, and their identity and role in the community were affirmed. Perhaps we now have the wisdom so to affirm the identity, role, and relationships of gay priests in our midst, to thank God for them, and to thank them for being on the threshold, conducting us, often fearfully, across the boundaries of corporate change into this new chapter in the world's story.

Of the many witnesses, within the Church and outside it, whom we could honour today, we have chosen James Baldwin, who died in 1987. He was neither Christian nor priest in any formal sense of the words, but if to be a priest is to discover the outcast in oneself and to embrace that figure, and so embrace all the oppressed, then James Baldwin was such a person. From accepting that identity, he moved outwards, through speaking and writing, through novels and tracts, through warm human loving, in anger and compassion for justice and freedom. Remembering him in the pages of *Gay Times* (4.88), the actor Martin Sherman wrote that his gayness was usually criticised or ignored by his contemporaries. They "would not, could not, deal with his gayness as a vital and enriching component of this man of rage and love, for it illuminated his blackness, and his blackness illuminated his gayness, and

together they enabled him to illuminate the fearsome laby-
rinth of the oppressed and the oppressor. He was a man of
illuminations. And the light consumed him."

8
Quotes?

From an advertisement for a male teacher in an all-boys' school:
[Assuming that such an advertisement is still legal!] He need not be gay. Some heterosexual men are good with boys, and we do not wish to discriminate.

An extract from a medical journal:
Patterns of sexual behaviour are varied. Don't assume, for example, that someone is heterosexual just because he or she is friendly with the opposite sex. It may be just a phase.

From an advertisement for a crack army regiment:
Gay couples are particularly welcome to apply. Our experience has shown that they encourage each other to deeds of gallantry and sacrifice that are all too rare these days.

A Civil Service memo:
Gay people in the Civil Service will not be discriminated against provided they are open about their sexuality and therefore not vulnerable to blackmail.

A member of an interviewing panel for prospective psychiatric nurses:
We find it hard not to discriminate in favour of gay people, for they have often reached a maturity and sensitivity which is much greater than that of their heterosexual contemporaries. They know only too well the dangers of a split life and of self-hatred, how these things can so easily lead to mental illness.

A bishop:
I have no hesitation in appointing an openly gay priest to be vicar of a parish. However, because I know how lonely a life that can be, I should prefer to appoint a gay couple who could

share the leadership of the church there. Jesus showed wisdom
and sensitivity when he sent his disciples out two by two, and in
the early days of the Salvation Army I understand that officers
were always appointed in pairs. Not that they were *all* gay, of
course – in a way, it's irrelevant. But if they happen to be, then
I can usually assume that they get on well together.

The senior partner in a group practice of doctors:
We *must* have someone gay to replace Jane. She was so good at
making sure gay people didn't come back for a second
consultation. I've never known anyone so able to convince
people that they weren't ill.

A representative of the 'Moral Majority':
We were wrong.

The Principal of a college of education to a student:
Thank you for telling me that you're gay. I appreciate the trust
you've placed in me. I'll write an even better reference for you
than I was going to do anyway. Your unusual courage and
honesty may do something to make up for what is lacking in
many a staff room.

A curate:
Of course! Gayness is much more the institution's problem
than it is mine. And I won't let it stop me from making
relationships any more. I've no need to live out other people's
fears.

From a Samaritans' Report:
Of the reasons given for people attempting suicide during the
year under review, that of homosexuality shows a dramatic
drop compared with five years ago. It is hard to know the
reasons for this, but we hope that the greater acceptance of gay
people by themselves and by society at large has done
something to keep them away from the borders of despair.

God:

I've been tempted to give up this Project Creation Earth recently and turn my attention to a less ambitious scheme. But you gay people have put new heart in me. You're showing up a lot of married couples by loving one another in a way that echoes deep within me – without controlling or possessing or using violence. You've been exploring the ways of love with great courage, and you've begun to stop trivializing yourselves in the process. Perhaps I'm on the right lines after all. . . .